K

Thanks for always giving me such great support about my writing.

With Love,
John

Lewis & Clark and me

Heading West from Travelers' Rest

by
John Crawford

With a Foreword by Dale A. Burk

STONEYDALE PRESS
PUBLISHING CO.

ISBN 1-931291-47-0
Library of Congress Control Number: 2005932309

STONEYDALE PRESS PUBLISHING COMPANY
523 Main Street • P.O. Box 188
Stevensville, Montana 59870
Phone: 406-777-2729

This book is dedicated to Max TeSoro, of Lolo, Montana, a young Lewis and Clark follower who, like myself, has caught the Lewis and Clark "fever", reading everything he can get his hands on about the 1803-1806 expedition. In the spring of 2004, Max was diagnosed with the need for a liver transplant. Although he has made a miraculous recovery from the surgery, he has experienced some setbacks.

When I told Max about the dedication and handed him the first two completed chapters, I immediately saw his eyes light up. If in some way this book can help Max in his recovery, then I will consider it a success.

Part of the proceeds from the sale of this book will go to help with his medical expenses.

COVER PHOTO:

John Crawford, shown at the "Woodman Meadows" overlook, with Woodman School and the approximate site of the Corps of Discovery's September 11, 1805 Woodman Camp in the background. Picture taken by Judy Crawford. All other photographs included in the book were taken by John Crawford on his journey.

Foreword

One persistent theme present in events surrounding the 200th anniversary of the Lewis & Clark Expedition is that of individuals everywhere along the trail projecting themselves into the adventure — of really, truly, wanting to have been there, of comprehending what it must have been like to have been along on that grand epic. To have shared in this wonderful adventure of exploration and discovery, and in the process realize a sense of personal achievement. Of making "their" story, "our" story.

There are, to be sure, opportunities along the Lewis and Clark Trail where one can convert these vicarious dreams into an on-the-ground reality, to literally follow in the exact footsteps of these intrepid explorers and get a sense of what it must have been like to "have been there." The key is that we not only find those places where that can happen but then to personalize the experience, to relate so intimately and profoundly to the details of the Expedition, to the point that a sudden realization comes upon you — and you mutter to yourself, "My God, this must have been what it was truly like to have been along on that grand epic."

Such is the case in this very personal essay by John Crawford. And how much more personal can you make it: "Lewis and Clark and Me." If that isn't self-projection into a story, what is? The crux of the story, however, is that John Crawford has put into action and words that impulse and passion that beats in each of us. His tale vibrates with the insights and words of personal involvement, of vitality, of comprehension and then understanding. Of relationships to the land and to the Corps. He takes us along, through words and deeds, into the very heart of a personal journey that the quality of his writing makes "our" journey.

Early in his book the author confesses to having been "caught up" in the Bicentennial fervor that swept the country, of reading the journals and collecting any sort of material he could on the Expedition, and then imagining what it would have been like to have been there. He tells of being "captivated" by the story, of a compulsion to "trudge" over mountain ridges and seeking echoes of the past, of pursuing proof that "they", meaning Lewis and Clark, "were still here". And then, in a profound insight, he brings us back to the realization that our endeavors to relive and recall and share in this history, ultimately, must remain vicarious. "I listened for some echoes of the past....but only the wind whispered a reply," he writes. Wow! That's good writing and it's typical of the quality of journey John Crawford takes us on throughout his book "Lewis and Clark and Me." My sentiment upon finishing this incredible book of a personal journey into the Lewis and Clark saga was that I had just completed a wonderful trip of my own, and that, if I could, I might retitle John's story to read "Lewis and Clark and Me, and Me Too." This is one of the better insights we've been given into this grand story and I trust that you'll enjoy it as much as I did.

Dale A. Burk
Stevensville, Montana
January 18, 2006

Acknowledgments

I am extremely grateful to my partner, Judy Crawford, who gave me editorial advice, encouragement, and support with "living out my dreams" of following in the footsteps of Lewis and Clark.

Thank you to my parents for instilling a "spirit of adventure" in me, and for their support of this book-writing experience, reading the chapters as fast as I could write them. Thanks, Mom, for using your proofreading skills to offer important edits to my book.

A big thanks to Carol and Rich Massat, my sister and brother-in-law, who encouraged me every step of the way through this book-writing process. Also, thanks to my brother, Jeff, who has joined me on many hiking, biking, and camping trips throughout the years, helping to fulfill both of our yearnings for adventure. To all my friends who cheered me on as I wrote this book, I offer my most sincere thanks.

Although my Grandmother Crawford passed away in 1988, the memories of her "Thoreau-like" descriptive letters about her Hill's Lake cottage in central Wisconsin were an inspiration for me to become an author.

I owe a special debt of gratitude to my niece, Becca Massat, who spent countless hours preparing my manuscript for publication.

I am extremely grateful to Robert Waugh, Tanna Paulson, and Henrietta Goodman for volunteering their time to proofread and edit my book.

My sincere appreciation to Dale Burk for putting his well-respected publishing name on my book, and for promoting, printing, and distributing ***Lewis & Clark and me...Heading West from Travelers' Rest****.*

A most sincere thanks to the Nez Perce and Salish tribes for answering my questions about the "K'uysey'ne'iskit" and "Naptnišá", the trails that their people have used for thousands of years.*

I acknowledge the efforts of the Lolo and Clearwater National Forests for implementing a policy of using a minimum of trail identification on the

* The spellings for both trails were obtained from the book, ***The Salish People and the Lewis and Clark Expedition***.

officially designated Lewis and Clark National Historic Trail and the Nez Perce (Nee-Me-Poo or Nimiipuu) National Historic Trail and other Native American trails, to achieve the maximum protection of the cultural resources. Thank you to Gene Thompson, Milo Mcleod, Kevin Foss, Le Ann Martin, and Carol Hennessey of the Forest Service for answering my questions about the historic trails.

Thank you to Shari Hayden, who gave me permission to hike on the Lolo Trail Ranch. Many thanks to the following people of the Travelers' Rest Preservation and Heritage Association, responsible for managing Travelers' Rest State Park: Loren Flynn, Executive Director, for the personal tour that gave my trip an informative beginning; Rob Collier, Native American Program Coordinator, and Darby Bramble, Program Coordinator, for helping to answer my questions about Travelers' Rest and the Lolo Trail. I appreciate all the other folks of the Travelers' Rest Preservation and Heritage Association, and the Lewis and Clark Trail Heritage Foundation—The Travelers' Rest Chapter and many other chapters across the country, for helping to preserve the rich Lewis and Clark and Native American history. Also, I'd like to acknowledge the time and efforts of the many volunteers at Travelers' Rest State Park, and all the other interpreters at the many visitor centers along the Lewis and Clark Trail for sharing in the colorful Lewis and Clark and Native American history across the land. A special thank you to Lem Mitchell, who works for the Clearwater National Forest as the cultural interpreter at Lolo Pass Visitor Center, for sharing his deep and colorful Nimiipuu roots with me.

Thank you to Dr. Harry Fritz, Chairman of the University of Montana Department of History, for answering my questions about the Lolo Trail. Thanks also to Francis Weigand, a Travelers' Rest volunteer interpretive guide, for reading my manuscript and checking it for historical accuracy.

Note from the author

One of my goals for writing **Lewis and Clark and Me...Heading West from Travelers' Rest** *is to make people more aware of the Lewis and Clark National Historic Trail and the Native American paths that it follows, to help ensure their protection. Native "peeled trees", I found out later in my journey, are called "culturally modified trees". Although most of these trees I found to be ponderosa pines, on follow-up visits to the historic trail I also discovered the Native Americans used the following species for food value: Douglas fir, western larch, whitebark pine, lodgepole, and cottonwood. Please respect the colorful Lewis and Clark and Native American history by protecting the evidence of their passing through this land.*

Although this book is not intended as a trail guide, if you plan to explore any of the Lewis and Clark Trail from Lolo, Montana, to Weippe, Idaho, make note that it is not a general-use type trail. The Forest Service has done limited work on the Montana side of the Bitterroot Divide in the Lolo valley—where the trail is only open to hikers—to help the public find the general location of the historic trail. East of Grave Creek, on Plum Creek Timber Company land, evidence of relatively "recent" tread (within the last fifty years) that parallels the historic tread, is fairly hard to find and has generally not been cleared of brush and downfall. In some areas the trail is closed to travel except by permission of the landowner. In Idaho, relatively recent-treaded Lewis & Clark Trail No. 25, that follows segments of the historic trails, is open to hikers and stock users in the area of Wendover Ridge and the Lolo Motorway.*

Lewis and Clark and Me...Heading West from Travelers' Rest *is threaded from beginning to end with quotes of Meriwether Lewis and William Clark. On my reenactment journey I refer to various books which have annotated versions of their quotes. For consistency, I have used the original Lewis and*

* The Forest Service requires the use of certified weed-free hay and/or pellets for stock, and recommends using weed-free feed at least 10 days prior to entering National Forests.

Clark quotes, taken from **The Definitive Journals of Lewis & Clark***, edited by Gary E. Moulton, a book I did not have during my journey. Quotes of Patrick Gass, an expedition member, were taken from* **The Journals of Patrick Gass***, edited and annotated by Carol Lynn MacGregor. The original journal notes of Lewis and Clark have poor spelling, which was reflective of that era. I make reference to the Nez Perce National Historic Trail in this book. Nez Perce is spelled "Nimiipuu" in the Native language. The historical trail markers blazed onto the west side of the trees to represent the "Flight of the Nez Perce" in 1877 have the English phonetic spelling of "Nee-Me-Poo" on them.*

Before you go along with me on my journey, I must admit that I do not consider myself a historian, only a lay person who finds western history fascinating. On my trip "through the Bitterroots", I followed the Corps of Discovery's and Native American route by comparing "the notes" in the journals with "clues" on the ground to find my way west from Travelers' Rest. My guesses about campsite and trail locations I do not present as historical facts.

Since my reenactment journey, a handicapped-access trail has been constructed to an overlook of a segment of the Pack Creek chain of meadows and a proposed site of the Corps of Discovery's Glade Creek Camp on September 13, 1805. Also since my reenactment journey, I have learned from the Forest Service that the following trail conditions have changed: a log footbridge with a railing has been constructed where the Lewis and Clark Trail crosses the West Fork of Lolo Creek, approximately three miles above Lolo Hot Springs; the West Fork of Lolo Creek to Packer Meadows Road trail section and the Howard Creek west trail section have better identification; and the Howard Creek east trail section has been completed to the Graves Creek Road. Check with the Lolo and Clearwater National Forests for current trail conditions and any permit requirements.

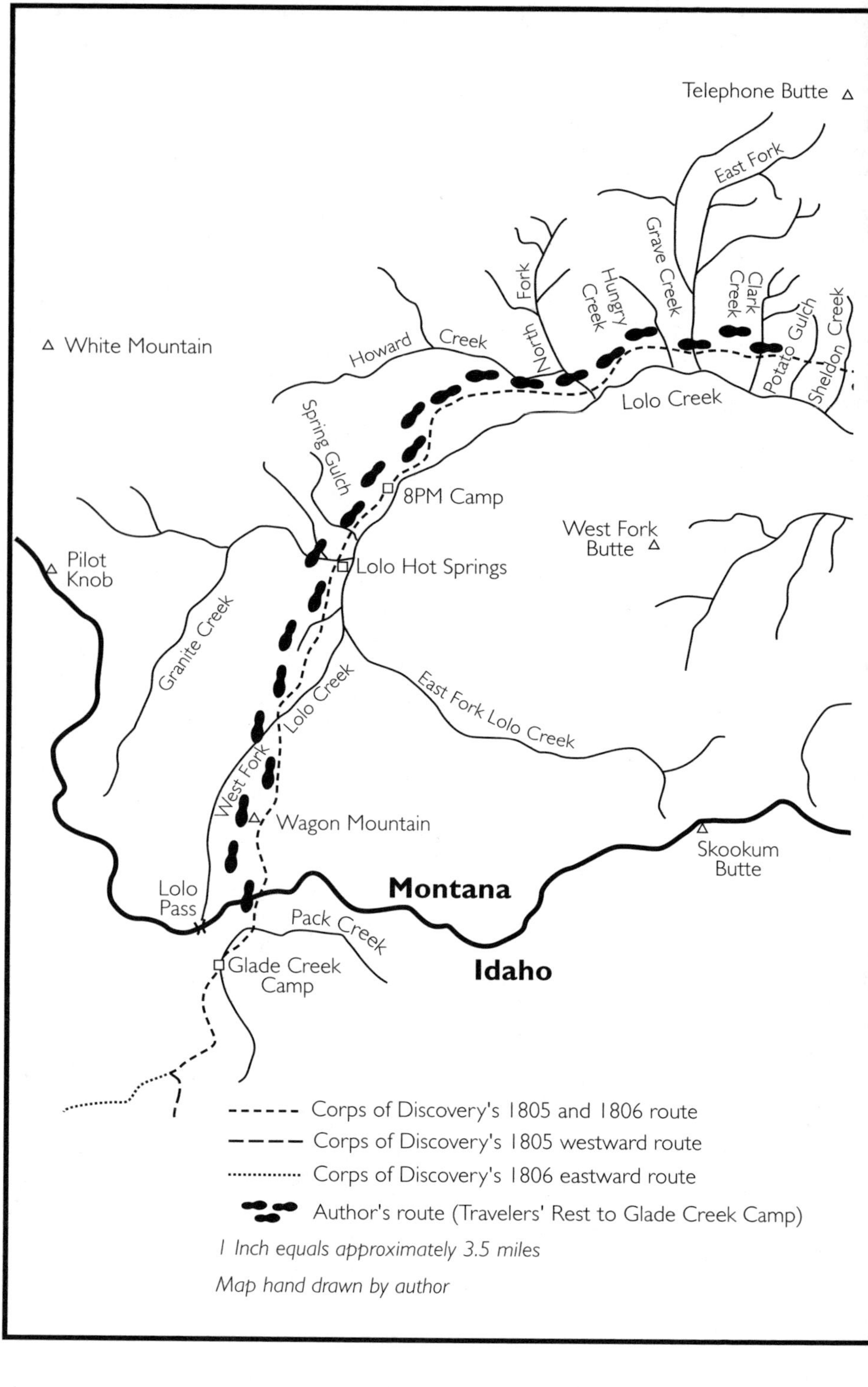

Telephone Butte
East Fork
Grave Creek
Clark Creek
Hungry Creek
North Fork
Potato Gulch
Sheldon Creek
White Mountain
Howard Creek
Lolo Creek
Spring Gulch
8PM Camp
West Fork Butte
Pilot Knob
Lolo Hot Springs
Granite Creek
East Fork Lolo Creek
Lolo Creek
West Fork
Wagon Mountain
Skookum Butte
Lolo Pass
Montana
Pack Creek
Glade Creek Camp
Idaho
Corps of Discovery's 1805 and 1806 route
Corps of Discovery's 1805 westward route
Corps of Discovery's 1806 eastward route
Author's route (Travelers' Rest to Glade Creek Camp)
1 Inch equals approximately 3.5 miles
Map hand drawn by author

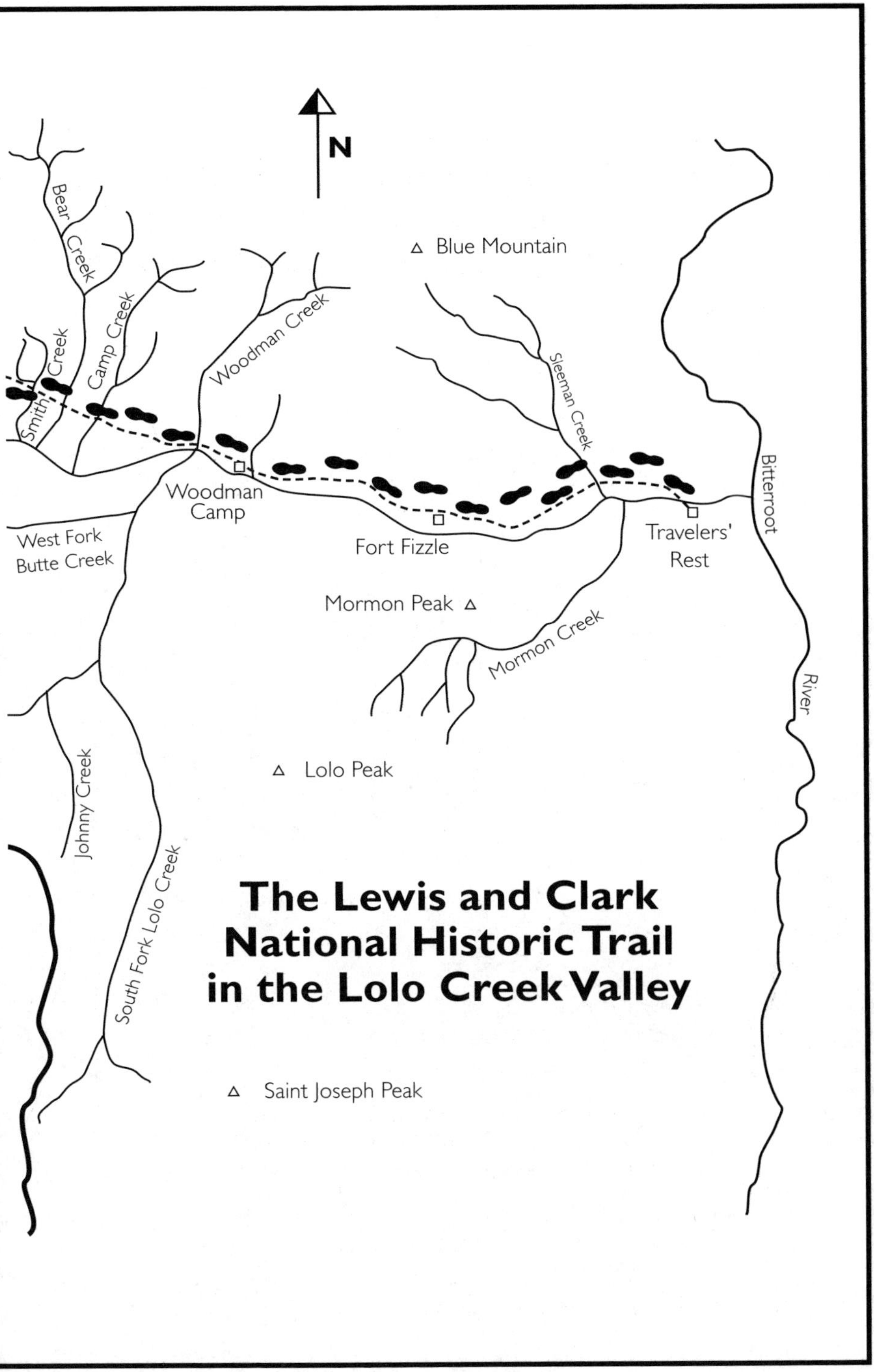

The Lewis and Clark National Historic Trail in the Lolo Creek Valley

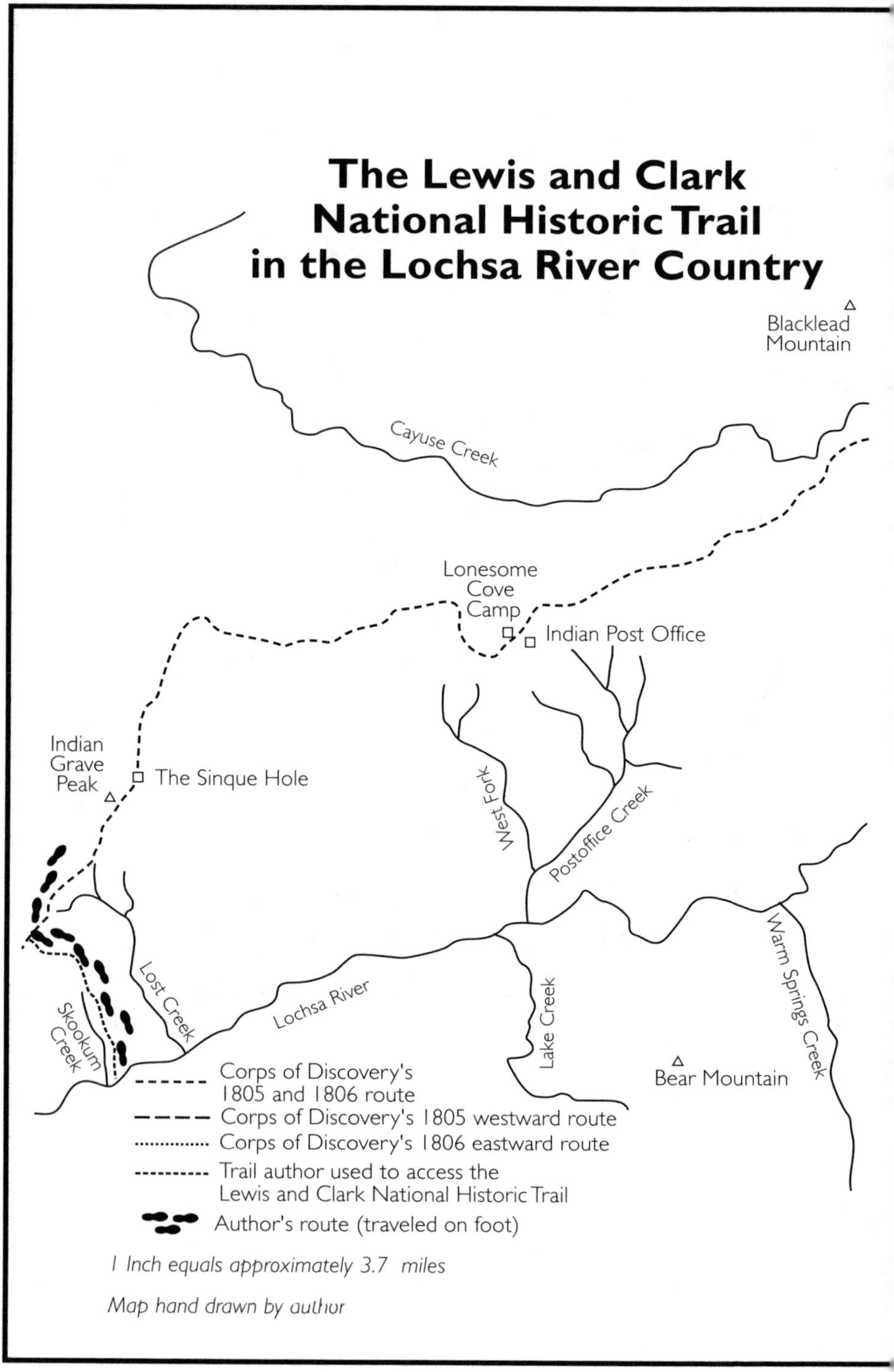
The Lewis and Clark
National Historic Trail
in the Lochsa River Country
Blacklead Mountain
Cayuse Creek
Lonesome Cove Camp
Indian Post Office
Indian Grave Peak
The Sinque Hole
West Fork
Postoffice Creek
Lost Creek
Lochsa River
Skookum Creek
Lake Creek
Warm Springs Creek
Bear Mountain
Corps of Discovery's 1805 and 1806 route
Corps of Discovery's 1805 westward route
Corps of Discovery's 1806 eastward route
Trail author used to access the Lewis and Clark National Historic Trail
Author's route (traveled on foot)
1 Inch equals approximately 3.7 miles
Map hand drawn by author

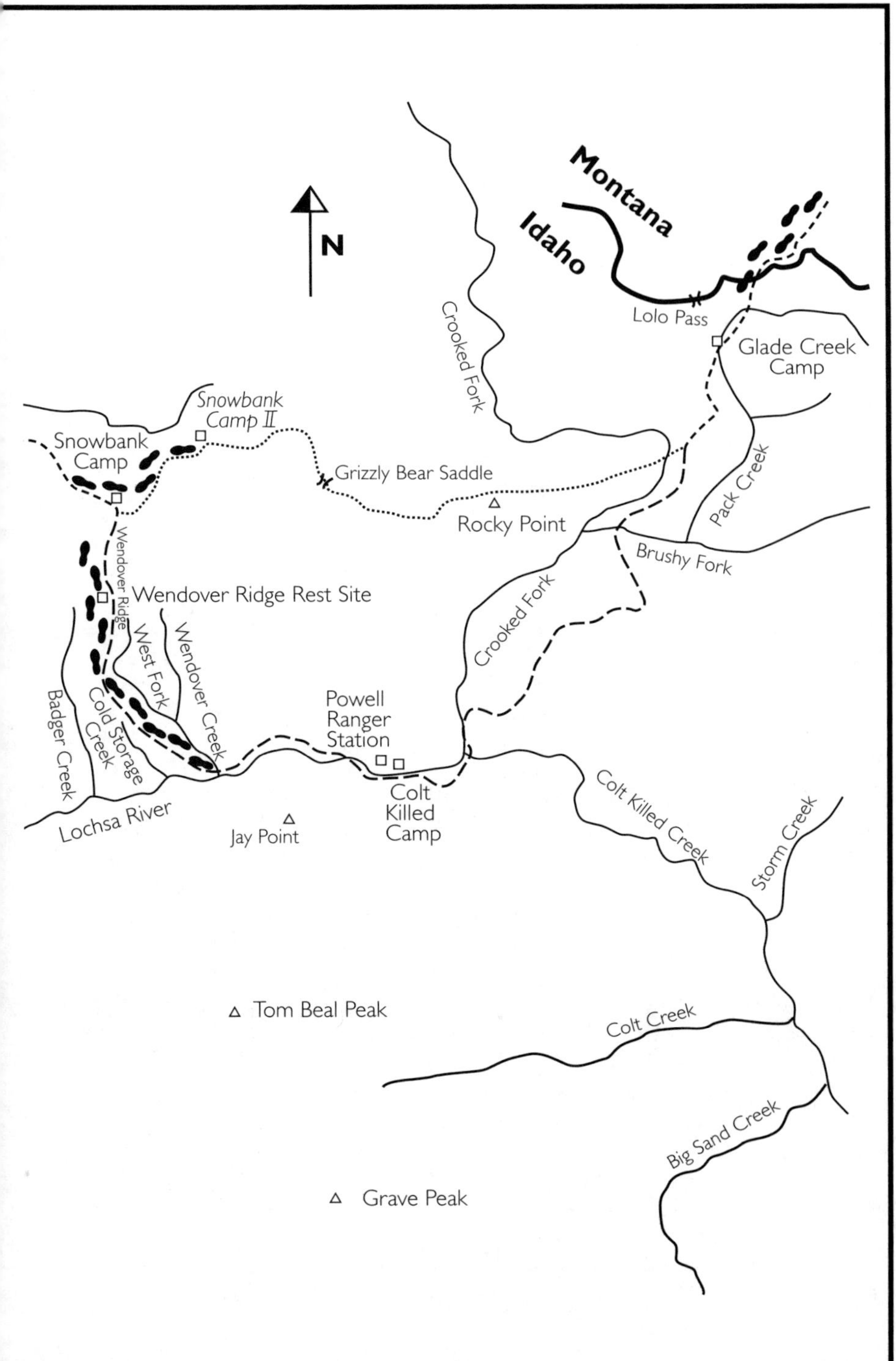
N
Montana
Idaho
Lolo Pass
Glade Creek Camp
Crooked Fork
Snowbank Camp II
Snowbank Camp
Grizzly Bear Saddle
Rocky Point
Pack Creek
Brushy Fork
Wendover Ridge
Wendover Ridge Rest Site
West Fork
Wendover Creek
Crooked Fork
Badger Creek
Cold Storage Creek
Powell Ranger Station
Colt Killed Camp
Lochsa River
Jay Point
Colt Killed Creek
Storm Creek
Tom Beal Peak
Colt Creek
Big Sand Creek
Grave Peak

Preface

The snow-covered mountains grew out of the dry Wyoming hills like some distant mirage drawing us to them. It was July 1967, and we were on the third day out of Wisconsin, on our second "out west" family vacation. Dad was the captain of our 1964 Ford station wagon, with serious concentration on the road, while Mom was navigating from the passenger seat. Then there were us kids, Carol, Jeff, and I, leaning over the back of the front seat, entranced by the steadily growing image on the far western horizon. Cookie, our pet collie, was wedged between us, her paws draped over the front seat, acting like she also was interested in what was showing in the front window picture screen.

A couple hours out of the Black Hills, I abandoned my watch of the mountains and brought out a handful of brochures we had collected in Sundance, the names of people and places of the west drifting along with us as we approached what Mom proclaimed were the Bighorn Mountains. In a flash the Bighorns were added to the list of places that shot out at me from those brochures: *Wall Drug, the Badlands, Mount Rushmore, Crazy Horse, Devils Tower, Little Bighorn, Pompeys Pillar, Virginia City, Yellowstone and Glacier Parks*. Then the names of colorful people of the "Old West" became bigger than life: *Buffalo Bill, Wild Bill Hickock, Calamity Jane, Butch Cassidy and the Sundance Kid*. I was enthralled by the pamphlets, absorbing the names of every western tourist site as if I were actually there, and waiting for every gunslinger to step out of the page and do a quick draw at this modern-day *alien* from the Midwest as we roller-coastered along, making our way over the low-slung hills, getting ever closer to the heart of the country that firmly held my interest in its grasp.

Dad drove into a scenic pullout outside of Buffalo, where we arched our necks looking up at the Bighorns that rose steeply out of a sea of small hills, standing guard to more hidden secrets of the west. Quickly we all bailed out, Carol, Jeff, and I running to the best vantage point, with Mom and Dad trailing behind. Like settlers in this majestic land, we stood in hushed awe at the mountains standing like huge snow-capped stone-carved monuments high above the valley floor. I could imagine climbing those mountains, exploring the craggy arms and deep hidden valleys, checking out the country that stood above Buffalo Bill Cody's old stomping grounds. After much too short a stop, we loaded up in our modern-day Conestoga station wagon and headed north toward Montana, eyes glued on the mountains that loomed off to our west.

It wasn't long after we had returned home to Wisconsin when I pulled out the brochures and spread them on my bed, making a collage of our trip with the snapshots that had arrived in the mail. Soon the feeling of "the west" came alive again, the memorabilia recapturing the unique aura of the places and characters that stared back at me like lures, drawing me back to the country west of the Missouri River.

I looked out my bedroom window, staring through the tentacle arms of the ancient oak trees that covered our Wauwatosa yard. Clarke Street stretched to the west, taking with it my desire to someday follow the road out of town, returning to the country I knew in my heart I had really never left.

It was December 28, 1973, when Judy, my new bride, and I put my plan of pulling up roots and moving west into action. Everything we owned got jammed into a fourteen-foot U-Haul trailer for the first leg of our journey. Quarter-size snowflakes dusted the oak leaves that covered the yard, with the forecast calling for blizzard conditions west of Milwaukee. We were heading into the guts of the storm, which was *perfect* weather for the type of western adventure I was seeking.

Sliding the U-Haul to a stop in Denver, we overwintered in the shadows of the Rockies, got jobs, and restlessly waited to make our next move. By spring we were like racehorses out of the gate—the '65 Chevy Impala loaded down with a couple weeks of supplies and camping gear—heading again into our unknown future, speeding north on I-25 into Wyoming, guided by some "inner compass". We drove past cities and towns with names that reeked of the Old West...Cheyenne, Laramie, and Rawlins, moving on to Muddy Gap, Lander, Crowheart, and Dubois. We traveled over Togwotee Pass, through the heart of the Grand Tetons and Yellowstone Park, then crossed into Idaho. Turning north at Boise, we drove through Cascade, McCall, and Grangeville. Then it was on to Kooskia and to Lowell, where we followed the Selway River to Fenn Ranger Station. There the Forest Service hired me for my dream-come-true job as a forest fire lookout on Indian Hill. For the next four months, we lived like the Swiss Family Robinson on a remote, isolated mountaintop at the edge of the Selway-Bitterroot Wilderness in a 14x14-foot all-glass house, sitting on top a forty-one-foot wooden tower, and withstanding everything nature could throw at us.

For over two decades we lived the primitive life of lookouts, returning like eagles to our nest perched high above the Selway River every fire season, to the place that we affectionately called our summer home. Then in the late 1990s, like a huge wave gathering force, the Lewis and Clark Bicentennial fervor grew in this country. I got caught up in it—reading the journals, collecting brochures, catching all the Lewis and Clark television and radio specials I could, and imagining where the historic trail passed by the house I had built in western Montana. By 2002, I had seen and heard enough. It was time to follow my "out west" adventure dreams even further, beyond the glass walls of the lookout house. My dreams would become boot tracks on the ground, where I would follow in the footsteps of the greatest explorers America has ever known.

Day 1

September 9, 1805

"we continued our rout down the W. side of the river about 5 miles further and encamped on a large creek which falls in on the West as our guide informes that we should leave the river at this place and the weather appearing settled and fair I determined to halt the next day rest our horses and take some scelestial Observations. we called this Creek Travellers rest."

—Meriwether Lewis

October 23, 2002

"Travellers rest." It was an appropriate place to begin my reenactment journey of following the Corps of Discovery's route through the Bitterroots to the Weippe Prairie in Idaho. This historical site was at the mouth of the Lolo Creek valley where Judy and I had made our home for over twenty years. It was the valley where Judy taught at a 110-year-old school, complementing my fire lookout job on Indian Hill where a vigil for forest fires had been going on for nearly a century. It was the valley where I built our western pioneer style, log-sided house.

The weather was clear and a brisk thirty degrees as I grabbed the mountain bike out of the bed of the pickup I had parked at the bike path trailhead along Highway 93, and started pedaling west for Travelers' Rest State Park. I replayed in my mind William Clark's journal entry of September 11, 1805…

"we Set out at 3 oClock and proceeded on up the Travelers rest Creek, accompanied by the flat head or Tushapaws Indians."

I glanced at my watch. 3:12. I picked up the pace, realizing I was running a little late to time my arrival at the historical site with the Corps of Discovery's *"3 oClock"* departure time.

I skidded to a stop in the loose pea gravel in front of the improvised garage visitor center. A sign read *Last tour will be at 3 p.m.,* deflating my excitement as quickly as a pinpricked balloon. Then my thoughts focused on the teeth-chattering cold wind blowing down the canyon I would have to bike through if I started my journey today. Sitting next to the wood stove and reading the Lewis and Clark journals instead of trying to *relive* them sounded a whole lot warmer. But then I thought about how much I had looked forward to this day when I could finally live out my dream of following Lewis and Clark. Undaunted by the cold and the wind, I marched like a long distant member of the Corps of Discovery to the house that served as the park headquarters, and knocked on the white-paneled door. *Tap tap tap…*

"Hi!" I announced to the dark-haired, thirty-ish looking man who suddenly appeared. "My name's John Crawford."

"I'm Loren Flynn, director of Travelers' Rest." Our hands met in a firm handshake.

"I was curious to see if I could still get a tour."

"Last tour was at three o'clock," he said matter-of-factly.

"Yeah, I read that on the sign," I replied, quickly trying to come up with something else to say to persuade him otherwise.

"We'll be giving more tours tomorrow," he added.

"Uh…but I'm starting out today on my journey following the Lewis and Clark Trail from here to Weippe," I explained as a cold breeze rattled the leaves from the large Chinese elm trees that stood guard around the green-shuttered, white two-story house. "And I'd sure appreciate it if you could give me a quick tour before I head out. I was trying to time the beginning of my trip with the Corps of Discovery's three o'clock departure on September 11, 1805. Guess I'm a little late." I shoved my hands in my pockets, crossing my fingers.

"Well…" he paused, pondering my request. "Yeah, I could give you a short tour."

"That would be fantastic!" I exclaimed, bubbling over with excitement.

"I'll meet you out by the garage."

"Sounds great! See you there!"

It was like magic—the feeling of standing next to the spot where Lewis and Clark, Sacagawea, Charbonneau, Old Toby, Colter, Gass, Ordway, Pryor, Drouillard, York, Cruzatte, Whitehouse, Shields, and the rest of the Corps of Discovery camped nearly two hundred years ago. Loren's excitement about Lewis and Clark history matched my own, as he told me about the discoveries of the spent .69-caliber musketball, military uniform pewter button, melted chunk of lead, and the blue bead. He explained that the park was part of a series of Native American villages that had stretched along the valley floor where evidence still remained of their old teepee rings. He talked about the discovery of mercury evidence found at the old latrine site from the Dr. Benjamin Rush's 700 mg mercury-laced pills the troops took as a laxative. Because the site fit the description of the order of encampment in Baron von Steuben's military manual, with the central cooking fire being within the "accepted distance" of where the pit should be dug, archaeologists had indeed uncovered conclusive proof that this was where the Corps of Discovery rested before heading into the Bitterroots in September 1805.

Loren's words flowed like the water of Lolo Creek, blending with the breeze rustling the dull yellow cottonwood leaves, keeping me captivated by his knowledge of every detail and every find at Travelers' Rest. Then, as if on some kind of command from the ghosts of Captain Lewis and Captain Clark for the tour to be over, his descriptions ended and my personal rediscovery tour started. After a quick snack at the picnic area in front of the makeshift headquarters, and another look at the journals, I was pedaling my way back to Highway 93, heading for the junction with Highway 12 where my journey would begin.

I thought about the logistics of following the Lewis and Clark Trail as I bicycled past my truck and made my way onto the concrete sidewalk on the west side of the four-lane highway. Locating the trail would require me to become a detective of sorts. Although the trail the Corps of Discovery followed had historical designation, and was the source of *Bicentennial fever*, except for segments of relatively recent tread it generally was not like a recreational trail that was well-marked, treaded, brushed, or cut out of downfall. From Travelers' Rest to the Weippe Prairie, it followed the route of the old Native American paths that were used for thousands of years before Lewis and Clark arrived on the scene in 1805. The Nez Perce called it "K'uysey'ne'iskit" or "Trail to the Buffalo Country", which they used to travel east to hunt bison. The Salish called it "Naptnišá" or "Trail to the Nez Perce", which they used to travel west to access the salmon fishing of the Lochsa, Clearwater, and Columbia Rivers. The trail was also used by the Native Americans to access areas to dig camas roots. Frequent use was also made of the trail by the Pend d'Oreille of western Montana. Occasional use of the trail was made by the Kootenai of western Montana, the Shoshone of the Lemhi Valley in Idaho, and the Columbia Plateau tribes of Washington and Oregon. Except for the relatively recent attempts by Forest Service trail crews to mark, cut out, and tread the general location of portions of the old trail, I was truly on my own *self-discovery* tour, following in the footsteps of those who went before me through this land, using the journals to find my way to the Weippe Prairie.

I pulled into Lolo Super Stop and got a cup of coffee to warm up, then started making bike tracks west on the officially designated Lewis and Clark Highway. Soon I approached the Lolo Trail interpretive sign I had practically memorized from past stops over the years, and continued to roll west, bucking the cold breeze that added to the wind blasts from the semi trucks, pickups, and sedans that sped by dangerously close to me. About a mile west of Lolo, I pulled up next to a Forest Service Fire Danger Rating sign at the base of a large rock outcrop, got off my bike and leaned it against the kickstand. I grabbed the journal from my pack and opened it to William Clark's September 11, 1805, entry...*"we Proceeded on up the Creek on the right Side thro a narrow valie and good road for 7 miles."* I noticed the old wagon road, which had been built to Lolo Hot Springs by 1888, going around the toe of the slope to the northwest. Using the trail clue, *"on the right Side,"* I figured the wagon road most likely followed the old Native *"road"* through this area, staying on the right or north side of the canyon to avoid the thick brush on the south side of the valley where most of the old creek braids were. Travelers' Rest was a good mile south of my location, and would have been more directly accessed by a short southeast spur trail branching off the main Nez Perce "Trail to the Buffalo Country". If my guess was correct, that meant Old Toby, their Shoshone guide, would have taken the Corps of

Discovery on a northwest tack on that spur trail out of Travelers' Rest, which would have had them meeting the main trail somewhere between Andrews Gulch and Sleeman Gulch. I stuffed the journal in my pack and continued west.

I stopped to check out the scene about a half mile west of the rocky bluff. Ponderosa pines and junipers dotted the dry hills that rose steeply out of the flat on the north side of the valley floor, with the old wagon roadcut at the base of the mountain ending where a grassy bench started. From there it looked like the wagon road followed the twenty-foot-high ledge a couple hundred feet south of the mouth of Andrews Gulch. Satisfied I was at, or close to, the place where they probably crossed to the north side of the valley, I checked for traffic, then pedaled west again.

"Hi there!" I yelled to the orange-vested man who was holding the *SLOW* sign by the side of the road where he watched for incoming and outgoing gravel belly dump trucks.

"Hi!" the flagger nervously answered back, surprised by my stealth presence as I coasted by mountains of gravel for the highway blacktop project.

"I'm following Lewis and Clark!" I yelled over my shoulder.

"Really?" I could tell his interest was lit.

"Yeah!" I instantly responded, continuing the over-my-shoulder conversation. "Well, better keep moving!"

"Have a good trip!"

"Thanks!" I yelled back, soon getting out of shouting range.

Two huge belly dumptrucks, rapidly approaching from the west, roared toward me as I leaned over, bracing for the approaching tunnel of air. ***Vrrr.....roommm!*** A huge gust of wind slammed into me as I vise-gripped the handle bars, struggling to stay in my foot-wide lane. The other gravel truck, following in its twin's wake, nearly swept me into the ditch. Cars and pickup trucks continued to sneak up from behind, their engines' whine increasing, building to a crescendo as they raced by, sending more short-lived hurricane gusts blasting into me.

A dark Mormon Peak shadow painted the pavement at mile three, where I entered the cold, biting, down-canyon wind, pulling to a stop at a side road. I got off the bike and dug into my pack for my winter parka to ward off the frosty air that was seeking every crevice in my thin nylon jacket. Across the highway, construction crews worked like a bunch of busy ants making their nest, trying to finish the soon-to-be convenience store "rest stop" for modern-day Lewis and Clark travelers.

Warm for the first time since entering the shade, I checked out the scene. Mormon Peak to the south, and the mountains to the north of the highway, formed a steep "V" notch in the canyon walls about a half mile to my west, constricting the valley from nearly a mile-wide flat to one that I could almost toss a rock across. Did the trail go through what was probably a brush-choked entryway or did it climb over the mountains to the north? I hopped back on my bike and pedaled northwest, riding up the private-residence access road to satisfy my curiosity. A half mile later at the end of Allen Lane, I was faced with a steep mountain that I felt nobody would go over no matter how much brush was in the canyon bottom. I backtracked to the modern-day *Traveler's Rest Country Store*, where I was met with the staccato of nail guns. A construction worker secured some green-metal roofing. A paving machine stood idle off to the side. I continued biking west beyond the construction zone, riding by a wind-rippled, ice-edged pond, its surface looking like a giant mirror casting wavy reflections of the golden aspen and cottonwood trees, the smell of decaying leaves drifting along with me.

At the Fort Fizzle interpretive site, about mile five, I absorbed the history of Lewis and Clark, the Nez Perce, and Captain Rawn. I was standing in the area where the Corps of Discovery traveled on their 1805 westbound and 1806 eastbound journeys. This was also the area where Captain Rawn and his troops had made log-sided rifle pits trying to stop the flight of the non-treaty Nez Perce who didn't want to move onto a reservation—a flight that started from their Native homeland of northeastern Oregon's Wallowa Valley in the spring of 1877. It was a collage of history, an intertwining of historical events, and it all happened here. I could *see* the troops in the rifle pits waiting for the Nez Perce coming from the west. I could also *see* the chiefs—Joseph, Ollokot, Looking Glass, White Bird, Toohoolhoolzote, and Hahtalekin—and the warriors, sitting proud on their horses along the ridges to the north, skirting around Captain Rawn and his troops with the women and children, the old and the wounded, escaping along what would become known as the Nez Perce (Nee-Me-Poo or Nimiipuu) National Historic Trail, going east in hopes of getting to Canada. Then I saw the Corps of Discovery traveling through, following the "Trail to the Buffalo Country" and the "Trail to the Nez Perce", with the question still perplexing me as to whether they took the valley route or the steep ridge route the Nez Perce used in 1877.

I let the trail location mystery settle to the back of my mind to solve on another day as I pedaled west, coasting by friends, neighbors, and families with children in the school where Judy taught. Clark wrote on September 11, 1805...

"we Proceeded on up the Creek on the right Side thro a narrow valie and good road for 7 miles and Encamped at Some old Indian Lodges, nothing killed this evening hills on the right high & ruged, the mountains on the left high & Covered with Snow."

Tonight I would "camp" at what I would call my *Travelers' Rest II*, resting at our house under *"the mountains on the left high & Covered with Snow."* Tomorrow I would continue my trek, going past more *"hills on the right high & ruged,"* and trying to locate where they had *"Encamped at Some old Indian Lodges."*

Day 2

October 24, 2002

I was late. Lewis and Clark had already been up and going.

Clark on September 12, 1805, writes…*"a white frost Set out at 7 oClock & proceeded on up the Creek."*

At 7 o'clock, white frost covered the rooftops. The temperature was seventeen degrees, much too cold for riding my bike along Highway 12. I studied the map, read the journals, and readied my daypack instead, patiently waiting for the thermometer on the porch to get above thirty.

By 12:30 the thermometer leveled off at twenty-eight degrees and I headed out, five and a half hours later than Lewis and Clark.

My ten-mile-per-hour pace created a brisk ten-mile-per-hour wind in my face as I pedaled west, closing in on the Corps of Discovery's *Woodman Camp*. Like yesterday, I passed more highway-confined old creek oxbows that used to extend to the *"hills on the right high & ruged,"* creating another Lewis and Clark mystery in my mind. Did the Corps of Discovery avoid the creek crossings by hugging the steep hillsides or did they ford the many crossings? I rode past familiar houses, barns, and sheds, pondering the question. The north canyon walls did appear too steep for them to have easily skirted around the creek crossings, and Lolo Creek would have been at a low water level in the fall of 1805. Most likely, I figured, they probably did ford the many stream crossings.

Suddenly the sound of a gravel truck approaching from the east triggered survival instincts as I squeezed the hand brakes and skidded to a halt in the graveled berm just to the west of Woodman School. I jumped off my bike and dropped into the ditch, leaning over to brace myself for the windstorm. ***5…4…3…2…1…***The blast of cold air tore into me as I stayed hunkered down, waiting for the wind gust to subside. I looked to see if the coast was clear, then dug the journals out of my daypack and reread the scene Clark described on September 11, 1805…

"we Proceeded on up the Creek on the right Side thro a narrow valie and good road for 7 miles and Encamped at Some old Indian Lodges, nothing killed this evening."

This description seemed to place their first night's camp out of Travelers' Rest somewhere near the little white school buildings that stood above me on a grassy bench at the base of a hill to my northeast. The *"7 miles"* though, did add some mystery to the camp location. The school where Judy taught was actually eight miles from Lolo. Clark's September 12, 1805 journal entry gave me more clues…

"Set out at 7 oClock & proceeded on up the Creek, passed a Fork on the right on which I saw near an old Indian encampment a Swet house Covered wthh earth, at 2 miles assended a high hill & proceeded through a hilley and thickly timbered Countrey…"

A short *"2 miles"* to my west was the end of the flat cattle pasture that Ralph Space referred to in his book, ***The Lolo Trail***, as *"Woodman Meadows."* That most likely was where the Corps *"assended a high hill,"* leaving the broad valley floor to enter the mountains. Woodman Creek, which I interpreted as the stream they crossed soon after departing their *Woodman Camp,* was the only sizable north-side-of-the-valley *"Fork on the right"* in the area. Assuming that Clark's *"7 miles"* reference was just slightly underestimated, the rest of the journal clues seemed to indicate their campsite was between Woodman Creek and Woodman School, probably close to the winding waters of Lolo Creek, southwest of the school. Ralph Space placed their camp *"about one half mile east of Woodman Creek."* I continued to prop up my bike, standing ten feet off the highway, and listened to the rush of the creek, the mooing of cattle, and the building storm of another fully loaded belly dumptruck heading my way. Ten seconds to the wind blast. Five seconds. The whirlwind collided into me as the loud vibrations of the truck engine and eighteen wheels rumbled west. I waited out the brief storm, then merged back onto the highway.

Passing Woodman Creek and the ranch buildings that now stood at the old Woodman townsite*, I kept my eyes out for any signs of the *"Swet house Covered wthh earth,"* but saw none, as the mound of earth most likely had eroded away after all these years. I continued along the modern-day blacktopped straight stretch beyond the Elk Meadows Road turnoff, paralleling the historic trail and wagon road route to the west end of *Woodman Meadows,* where I coasted to a stop, bringing out the journals again. Clark wrote on September 12, 1805...

"at 2 miles assended a high hill & proceeded through a hilley and thickly timbered Countrey for 9 miles & on the Right of the Creek, passing Several branches from the right of fine clear water..."

According to the journals, I was now at the end of the relatively easy valley route, and beginning the Corps of Discovery's tough trip "through the Bitterroots". According to the map, the Corps would not follow the valley bottom anymore except for a short section by the State highway station, just below Lolo Hot Springs. The wagon road and old trail were diverting here, with the double-rut road staying low in the valley, taking the more direct route to the hot springs; and the old Native American buffalo and salmon trail climbing into the mountains to avoid the thick brush and many stream crossings in the canyon bottom. I scoped out the location where the Lewis and Clark Trail left the north side of the valley floor and *"assended a high hill."* The easiest route to the hills appeared to be up a small ravine just to the north of some ranch buildings. The old, half-fallen-over Erickson log cabin† grew out of the ground at the mouth of the ravine, looking like a gate of entry where the Corps *"proceeded through a hilley and thickly timbered Countrey."*

I contemplated what to do next. The Forest map showed the trail making a major diversion from the valley floor, leading into a mosaic of

* Established in the 1880s, the town of Woodman, located on the old Woodman homestead, was a logging, ranching, and mining community, and a stage stop for travelers between Lolo and Lolo Hot Springs. Woodman's population swelled to over 500 residents during the surveying for a possible railroad route between Lolo, Montana and Kooskia, Idaho, which was done around 1908. When plans for the railroad were scrapped, the town was practically deserted overnight. With a decrease in mining activity and the advent of the automobile replacing the need for the stagecoach, Woodman essentially became a ghost town by 1916. At its height, Woodman had a post office, a number of saloons, and a store. The 1902 Woodman Schoolhouse, built about a mile to the east of the town, is considered to be the last remaining landmark of the townsite.

† This two-story log cabin is one of the last remaining buildings from the Ole Erickson Ranch of the early 1900s.

private land ownerships which continued west to Grave Creek. Gene Thompson, of the Lolo National Forest, had informed me of his uncertainty about whether this portion of the historic trail was marked with ribbon or had any recent-made tread similar to what the Forest Service had done on their land west of Grave Creek. My thoughts drifted back through the years to the Corps of Discovery's tough trip through the same Bitterroot Mountains through which I would be passing. Snow had already fallen in the high country as Clark had described on September 11, 1805… *"the mountains on the left high & Covered with Snow."* To the south of me, the 9,096-foot Lolo Peak stood high and covered with a thin wintry blanket, much as it must have looked to Clark nearly two hundred years ago. But I was well over a month later in the calendar year on my journey than they had been in 1805, when William Clark wrote on September 16, 1805…

"began to Snow about 3 hours before Day and Continud all day the Snow in The morning 4 Inches deep on The old Snow, and by night we found it from 6 to 8 Inches deep I walked in front to keep the road and found great dificuelty in keeping it as in maney places the Snow had entirely filled up the track, and obliged me to hunt Several minits for the track." Clark went on to explain… *"I have been wet and as cold in every part as I ever was in my life, indeed I was at one time fearfull my feet would freeze in the thin mockersons which I wore."*

The journal entries convinced me to leap-frog ahead and leave the fairly low elevation *Woodman Meadows* to Grave Creek section for a later date. For now I had to make fast tracks through the high country to get to the Weippe Prairie before the winter snows would close down my journey for the year. I hopped back on the mountain bike and continued to make my way west on the right side of the white-painted line.

About mile twelve, I pedaled into shadow-covered blacktop, instantly feeling the chill in the air. A thin layer of black ice formed on the pavement as I entered dangerous bike-riding territory, going into the *many-bends-in-the-highway* section west of Bear Creek. Like floating a Class VI section of river, I was headed into a life-and-death section of highway for bike riders.

Danger was lurking as a caravan of three eighteen-wheelers headed straight for me into the tightest of the ten bends in the narrow roadway. I said a little prayer for survival as the first truck nearly blew me into the guardrail. Prayer answered. Truck number two created another windblast that *almost* caused me to do a header over the guardrail. *Fear* swept over me when I heard the jake-brake vibrations split the air from yet another fully loaded gravel truck bearing down on me, this one from behind. Three seconds to the meeting of the eastbound and the last of the westbound trucks, and possibly one scrunched-to-the-guardrail bike rider. ***3…2…1…*** The trucks' wakes collided, eddying past the gray-sided semi trucks going in opposite directions, as I kept my head down and a firm grip on the handlebars to prevent the bike from another near collision with the guardrail. I quickly pedaled through the last two bends before any more trucks arrived on the scene, with the peaceful rippling of Lolo Creek returning, and my heart finally dislodging from my throat. At the Lolo Creek Campground, I breathed a huge sigh of relief and took a break.

On a wooden bridge two hundred feet off the highway, I finally felt safe. Occasional waves of traffic whizzed by my safety zone as I ate my lunch and studied the map. The Clark Creek drainage lay to the northeast across the highway, an area where the trail would have to remain a mystery until I got back from the Weippe Prairie. I sipped on some water from my green-tinted Nalgene plastic bottle and absorbed the scene, listening to the peaceful gurgling of the thirty-foot-wide creek as it slipped over melon-size rocks. Clark's September 12, 1805 entry described the trail section north of the highway…

"The road through this hilley Countrey is verry bad passing over hills & thro' Steep hollows, over falling timber &c. &c. continued on & passed Some most intolerable road on the Sides of the Steep Stoney mountains, which might be avoided by keeping up the Creek which is thickly covered with under groth & falling timber."

Anxious to get to the *"Sides of the Steep Stoney mountains,"* and off the *too-narrow-of-a-highway* for safe bike riding, I quickly finished my lunch and merged back into the foot-wide lane, pedaling as fast as I could for the Howard Creek Trailhead.

Three more miles of belly dumptruck *Russian Roulette* and I was finally at the beginning of my dayhike that would take me east on a round trip to Grave Creek and back. I locked my bike to a tree, read the interpretive signs, strapped on my daypack and headed out.

But where *did* the trail start? Another interpretive sign on the west side of the Howard Creek Road described a loop trail that followed a portion of the Lolo Trail, which included the Lewis and Clark Trail and the Native American trails, taking off to the right of the sign. I could see the obvious path the sign described disappearing into the thick woods along Howard Creek. I also noticed the path at the other end of the loop trail coming down a steep grade to the left, behind the sign. I would head west on that path tomorrow morning. But the eastbound trail was nowhere in sight. *"You go across the creek and up the road a short ways to find the trail heading east,"* I recalled the Lolo National Forest receptionist telling me.

Over the culverted creek I marched, looking for the trail that took off to the right. Nothing showed until I was about two hundred feet up the Howard Creek Road, where I discovered Lewis and Clark National Historic Trail and Nez Perce (Nee-Me-Poo) National Historic Trail markers and obvious tread heading east. "Hooray!" I yelled into the thickly treed forest. I was finally stepping on the Lewis and Clark Trail that followed the "Trail to the Buffalo Country" and the "Trail to the Nez Perce". I also would be following a good portion of the Nez Perce Trail, identified with historical markers blazed onto the west side of the trees, which represented the Nez Perce's 1877 eastward flight from Captain Howard. Lewis and Clark National Historic Trail markers blazed onto the east side of the same trees, represented the Corps of Discovery's 1805 westward journey to the Pacific Ocean. It finally was all happening…the pieces to the *Go West Young Man* game I played in my mind as a kid were becoming *my tracks* on the ground.

The romanticism of taking this trail, though, soon changed after a walk-in-the-park easy hike through a thick, mature forest of lodgepole, spruce, fir, and larch led to a difficult climb out of Howard Creek, as I huffed and puffed my way up a steep ascent that definitely was not following any Forest Service trail-construction guidelines. A quarter mile into my Lewis and Clark trek, with about 145 miles to go, I was already convinced I wasn't in shape for what lay ahead.

I took a breather and reread the journals… *"passed Some most intolerable road on the Sides of the Steep Stoney mountains."* Clark's words rang true as I continued my climb straight up the flank of the *"Steep Stoney"* mountainside.

The trail didn't go to the ridgetop as I thought it would, but instead ended up contouring across the slope, with a short downhill stretch which led to an overlook of the old Lolo Work Center. Then another steep uphill climb was followed by a steep downhill descent and more contouring of the slope as the trail roller-coastered its way east through a Douglas fir and ponderosa pine forest.

The memorized description from Clark's journal of *"Steep hollows, over falling timber &c. &c."* was another ditto for the country I was hiking over. But what was the *"&c. &c."* all about? Maybe it had something to do with the uprooted tree wells I was finding, which looked like an F-16 had just finished a bombing mission in the area. It also might have referred to traveling through this *"Steep Stoney"* country in thin moccasins. I had the best hiking boots money could buy, made by Merrill, soled by Vibram for good traction, with stiff leather for lateral stability, and Gortex-lined to make them waterproof. The Corps of Discovery had moccasins made of buffalo and deer hide, which definitely were not waterproof, with absolutely no lateral stability or any kind of traction on the *"Sides of the Steep Stoney mountains."*

As I headed east, variegated orange, cream, and gray rock outcrops started to appear out of the mountain's skin, dotting the steep fir-and-pine-covered mountain slopes. About a mile out from the trailhead I made a descent into a steep, waterless ravine that was perched just above the highway and crowned by old-growth western larch, Douglas fir, and Engelmann spruce. I stared up at the stately giants in the tucked-away, perched valley, suddenly feeling quite small. Soon I left the cold, damp, frosty bench of stately tree sentinels and started a steep climb up a dry, rock-outcropped mountain of pine and fir.

After hitting a high point on the trail, I began contouring to the east. Suddenly *something* moved off to my left, upslope, about two hundred feet away! I stopped and scoured the dusk-colored, leafless brushy mountainside, but nothing showed. Was I seeing things? I kept up my vigil for the *phantom* predator, remembering that my bear spray was hidden deep in my pack. *Whatever it was* would have to wait to attack until I could take off my pack, grab the pepper spray, and then read the instructions on the can. Figuring that distance was my best defense against the invisible animal, I got the heck out of there, jogging east.

Within a couple hundred yards I exchanged my jog for a crawl, every step measured as I carefully made an extremely sharp descent along the side of some cliff faces terracing the mountain above a hidden elevated valley. Holding onto vegetation, I made my way down into a special grotto of rock ledges draped with moss, brush, and small trees sheltering the foot-wide creek that oxbowed through the frosty, brushy, grass-covered basin. A soft trickling massaged my senses as I watched the satiny thread of water slip between two narrow ribbons of crystal thin ice, making its way through the alder, redstem ceanothus, and mountain maple brush, disappearing under an old moss-covered log and into a small pool where the trail crossed the creek. Too damp and cold to stay for long, I reached down for a cupped handful of water and drank, then headed up the steep slope to the east.

Like going through a stone gate, I climbed between rock outcrops when I reached a prominent point on the divide above the creek basin. Just to the east and uphill of the "gate", a large rock monolith rose about forty feet out of the mountain above the trail, looking like a giant orange-and-white layer birthday cake, crowned with a lone twenty-foot fir tree serving as the candle.

In the middle of an old logging unit, my eyes were drawn to a huge old gray-weathered tree that lay in its permanent burial site, stretched out onto the soft carpet of vegetation to the high side of the trail. There was something about that ancient tree, something I remembered from the journals. Excited, I dug out my copy of the nearly two-century-old logbook and paged forward to more of Clark's entry of September 12, 1805… *"on this roade & particularly on this Creek the Indians have pealed a number of Pine for the under bark which they eat at certain Seasons of the year, I am told in the Spring they make use of the bark."* I waded through the knee-high grass to the fallen tree and checked out the carved edges that formed a rough four-foot-long triangle enclosing a charred black section of wood. Like an arrowhead, the ancient-looking cut had scalloped edges, hatchet- or knife-carved by the Native Americans who had peeled the outer bark to expose the inner cambium layer they would eat in the spring of the year. I continued to stare at the tree, letting the Native American history absorb into my soul.

As I climbed the steep trail out of the unusually flat bench of the old logging unit, I thought back to my pre-trip visit with Gene Thompson, when he told me that where the recent Forest Service cut trail wasn't completed yet, brown-and-orange striped flagging and the Lewis and Clark Trail and Nez Perce (Nee-Me-Poo) Trail historical markers would help guide me through the country. On the Idaho side, he said that large segments of the historic trail were unmarked, making these sections nearly impossible to find. If I was observant enough, I felt I might also be able to use the wood-carved evidence of the peeled trees as trail blazes, which could help guide me on my trip through the Bitterroots.

I went through another rock outcrop "gate" where the trail topped out, then started a steep descent into the bottom of Hungry Creek. Similar in size to the creek in the unnamed drainage I had passed a mile back, the narrow, ice-edged, silvery thread dove over a small ledge into a tiny pool, then slithered through a grassy flat under clumps of alder and a large gnarly-armed nasty-thorned hawthorn tree, making its way toward Lolo Creek. I jumped over the frozen banks and came to a logging road just off the highway behind a locked gate. After a fruitless search for the trail heading east to Grave Creek, the increasing shadows over the mountains prompted the decision to turn around a mile from my goal. Disappointed, I jumped back over Hungry Creek and carefully made my way past the hawthorn tree that stood guard over the tranquil stream, initiating the three-mile backtrack to Howard Creek and my prearranged shuttle pick-up by Judy. Making my way back west, I returned on the "recent" trail tread over the *"Steep Stoney mountains"* and the *"Steep hollows, over falling timber &c. &c.,"* getting a double dose of what the Corps of Discovery experienced on September 12, 1805.

As night's curtain fell upon the land, Judy and I drove back to our home and my *Travelers' Rest II* to get ready to head west from Howard Creek in the morning.

Indian Hill Lookout…where our "out-west" adventure began in 1974.

Getting ready to leave Travelers' Rest on my reenactment journey. (TOP) *Improvised garage visitor center at Travelers' Rest State Park, October 23, 2002.* (BOTTOM)

Passing Woodman School while biking along the Lewis and Clark Highway. (TOP) *West of Woodman School, looking northwest toward "toe-of-the-slope" historic trail route.*(BOTTOM)

Woodman Creek, Clark's "Fork on the right".

Steep trail section east of the Howard Creek Trailhead.

Recent trail tread about a mile west of the Howard Creek Trailhead. (TOP LEFT) *Rock outcrops west of the Howard Creek Trailhead.* (TOP RIGHT) *At the saddle above Howard Creek where the trail disappeared.* (BOTTOM)

Uniquely carved culturally modified tree. (TOP) *About four miles west of the Howard Creek Trailhead, where I bushwhacked my way to the trail in the saddle at the right of the picture.* (BOTTOM)

Along Highway 12 just east of the vicinity of the Corps of Discovery's 8 PM Camp. (TOP) *Logging road where the trail comes out about a half mile east of the Corps' 8 PM Camp.* (BOTTOM LEFT) *Heading west from the trailhead on the Fish Creek Road.* (BOTTOM RIGHT)

Lewis and Clark National Historic Trail marker on the east side of tree to represent the Corps of Discovery's 1805 westward journey.

Nez Perce (Nee-Me-Poo) National Historic Trail marker on the west side of tree to represent the eastward 1877 "Flight of the Nez Perce".

My "little brother", Carl Johnston, at the Lolo Hot Springs pool.

Rock cairn marking the trail in logging unit northeast of Wagon Mountain.

Iced-over log I used to cross the West Fork of Lolo Creek.

The area where the trail disappeared on climb out of the canyon toward Wagon Mountain. (TOP) *The trail going through a logging unit south of Wagon Mountain.* (BOTTOM)

Where I lost the trail in the logging unit south of Wagon Mountain.

"Elevated puncheon" constructed by the Forest Service south of Wagon Mountain to protect the riparian area.

Log foot bridge constructed by the Forest Service at the head of the West Fork of Lolo Creek. (TOP) *The last in the chain of meadows along Pack Creek where I guessed was the location of the Corps of Discovery's Glade Creek Camp.* (BOTTOM)

Searching for the historic trail just southwest of where I placed the Glade Creek Camp. (TOP) *Site of Corps of Discovery's Colt Killed Camp, where they "Encamped oposit a Small Island" (in left background).* (BOTTOM)

"Whitehouse Pond", which Joseph Whitehouse made reference to in his journal, located just east of the Wendover Ridge Trailhead.

Day 3

October 25, 2002

It was a clear, crisp twenty-two degrees shortly after 8 a.m. when I parked my truck and started heading west from the Howard Creek Trailhead, continuing on what Clark described on September 12, 1805, as, *"...Some most intolerable road on the Sides of the Steep Stoney mountains, which might be avoided by keeping up the Creek which is thickly covered with under groth & falling timber."*

Sweating my way up the *"Sides of the Steep Stoney mountains,"* I stopped at the first gentling of the grade at an overlook about a mile west of the trailhead. Western larch trees dotted the mountainsides, dabbing gold into the deep green fir and pine forests that dove into the valley floor, forming overlapping V's to the distant ridges on the western horizon. Rock outcrops grew out of the mountainsides like a bunch of huge stalagmites, enticing me to climb them and peer over their thirty-foot drop-offs. Then I *felt* the dizzying heights, the *invisible* force pushing me off the cliffs, the *vertigo*. Wisely I gave up on any climbing ideas, and continued hiking past the miniature rock towers.

I hiked up the steepening trail through an old-growth ponderosa pine and Douglas fir tree park with another mystery unfolding. Old trail braid trenches in the mountainslope shadowed the new Forest Service tread. Could it be that the Native Americans followed not one path, but many? Maybe the Native trail was actually a series of trails.

Climbing onto an old logging road that formed a bench on the ridge dividing Lolo Creek from Howard Creek, I rested and gazed out to the north at larch trees that looked like thousands of candles lighting up the valley. I guessed that I was about three miles west of the trailhead, with the map showing I would come out at the Lolo Creek valley floor near the Montana Highway Department buildings, which were approximately another six miles to my west. Nothing but more mystery stared at me, as the obvious tread that led into the saddle showed no indication of continuing beyond the divide. I took a self-timed picture of myself, drank some water, and began a search for some sign of the missing trail.

After beating through the brush for five minutes, I quickly realized that the vanishing trail tread and missing historical markers were no mirage, as the saddle definitely was the turn-around spot for most dayhikers. Soon, though, I started seeing a faint trail, and more importantly, some brown-and-orange striped flagging. With my good woods sense, I felt even if I couldn't find tread, I would still be able to discover the route by following the flag line. But soon I lost the trail again, and there were no more flags dancing in the wind that had started to breathe across the ridge. I wandered over the mountain, looking for some sign of the trail; then, like magic, the narrow path appeared within a group of small pine trees. More striped ribbon and peeled tree discoveries proved I hadn't strayed too far.

More patterns started to form, putting together the pieces of the puzzle of why the Native Americans might have put the trail where they did. It seemed that if the slopes weren't too brushy, they stayed midslope, diving the tread into steep ravines and climbing out the other side, not bothering to go to the heads of the canyons. But if the brush was thick, they put the trail higher in the creek basins, using the ridge routes.

Around mile four, when I crossed into the Howard Creek drainage, I lost all signs of the trail again. From a vantage point I could see a prominent mountain off to the northwest, about two miles away. My instincts told me to head for the obvious saddle that lay about halfway between that mountain and my location. After bushwhacking for half an hour I arrived at the saddle, reconnecting with the tread, proving that my pathfinding instincts were correct. As I headed out of the pass, cairns started to appear, looking like miniature stone monuments along the side of the trail.

About mile six, I stopped for another break, and sat in a clump of beargrass in an old logging unit. I got out my water bottle, brought out the map and trail mix, and peered out over the Lolo valley. The winding waters of Lolo Creek lay hidden from view, nestled far below me. Lolo Peak, on the southeastern skyline, stood as a nine-thousand-foot sentry guarding the northern end of the jagged Bitterroot Mountains' crest. The tiny white West Fork Butte Lookout building capped the fir-and-larch-covered mountain across the valley in front of the taller peaks. A larch-dotted evergreen ridge just off to the southwest blocked my view of the area of the highway station, where Ralph Space, in his book ***The Lolo Trail***, placed the Corps of Discovery's *8 PM Camp*. Clark's journal of September 12, 1805, noted…

"Crossed a mountain 8 miles with out water & encamped on a hill Side on the Creek after Decending a long Steep mountain, Some of our Party did not git up untill 10 oClock P M. I mad camp at 8."

The *"8 miles"* from Howard Creek, the last significant water source, slightly undershot what I guessed to be about nine miles to where they arrived at or near the valley floor, after they ended up *"Decending a long Steep mountain."* Where they *"encamped on a hill Side on the Creek"* was a little perplexing to me, as there were many camping flats below the hot springs along Lolo Creek. The *"mad camp at 8,"* though, was a clue they probably arrived at their campsite near dark, and the *"10 oClock PM."* arrival time for the rest of the party probably would have made it impractical for them to have searched for a more suitable spot than an uncomfortably sloped hillside. Where that *"hill Side"* was only added to the mystery of the Lewis and Clark Trail.

I studied the Forest map, which showed the segmented line of the approximate route of the *"Lewis & Clark Trail"* cutting across the head of an unnamed drainage just to the west. From there it veered south and dove straight down a ridge to the highway shed. I put away the map and absorbed the heat of the sun-warmed clearing, with the pale-green beargrass and golden grass tickling my exposed skin. It was 1 p.m. The sun had already peaked and started its descent toward the west horizon. Time was getting to be a factor if I still planned on hiking to the *8 PM Camp* and beyond to the Lolo Hot Springs trail section. The wind blew across the clearing, shivering the grasses, waving the tops of the fifteen-foot pine and fir trees and rustling a lone aspen that hadn't lost all its leaves. I got up and continued heading west, contouring across a mountainside that was just as Clark described, *"with out water."*

Soon I lost all signs of the recent-made tread, following instead the Native braids and peeled trees that eventually led me back to the Forest Service trail that veered south, following the ridge that formed the eastern flank of the unnamed drainage. I wound my way down the steep mountain, continuing to lose the trail, then doing short searches to find it again, as I made my way onto a logging road that paralleled the unnamed creek and escorted me out to the freshly blacktopped Highway 12, a half mile east of the highway maintenance shed.

I hiked along the edge of the new pavement to just east of the highway department, where I stopped at a grassy flat crowned by a couple dozen golden-leaf aspen trees and replayed Clark's quote in my mind… *"encamped on a hill Side on the Creek."* Still baffled by the location of the *"hill Side"* campsite, I felt I was at least in the general area of their *8 PM Camp*. Clark's September 13, 1805 journal entry… *"I proceeded on with the partey up the Creek at 2 miles passed Several Springs,"* verified I was indeed close to the Corps of Discovery's camp, with that distance matching the approximate mileage to the hot springs. Suddenly I heard the distant sound of a gravel belly dumptruck building like thunder off to my east. The *storm* got closer and closer. Then the large truck rumbled past me, bringing with it a parade of pickups and sedans following a pilot truck. The noise slowly faded to the sound of aspen leaves singing in the breeze.

My trek took me a mile southwest of the highway station to an interpretive sign. Another pilot-truck-led parade rolled west, as I absorbed more Lewis and Clark history. Then a rig bore down on me, slowing, then stopping. I ignored *whoever it was*, concentrating instead on reading the sign. Someone opened a vehicle door, as I reached into my pocket and felt the bear spray trigger, ready to quick-draw my weapon like Doc Holiday practicing for a shootout at the OK Corral.

"Hi John!"

"Oh my gosh!" I gasped, my finger almost triggering the bear spray as I turned around and saw Kevin Conran, a long time Forest Service friend who lived and worked in southern Idaho. "What are you doing up in this neck of the woods?" We shook hands. "And how'd you know it was me, if you were coming from behind?"

"I recognized your walk!" he exclaimed. "Thought maybe you might have run out of gas somewhere."

I explained to my friend about my quest to find the Lewis and Clark Trail, then took up his invitation to ride the next mile to the start of the Lolo Hot Springs section. After a ten minute visit, Kevin continued heading west on the highway as I hiked northwest up the Spring Gulch Road, searching for brown-and-orange striped flagging, tread, historical markers, cairns, or any Native American peeled trees. By the second switchback on the graveled logging road, about a mile from the highway, my scavenger hunt for trail clues came up empty. But I *did* see an old skid trail taking off to the southwest, which I thought might tie in with the historical tread, so I took it. Within a half mile, the skid road gave out and I was hopelessly lost in the confusing, gently rolling terrain. Too lazy to take off my pack and read the map, I wandered cross-country through the maze of hills and valleys for about another mile until I topped out on a rise, noticing a creek that lay about a hundred yards to my south. A quarter mile off to my right a gravel road cut across the obscure valley, with a wooden bridge spanning the slow-moving peaceful mountain stream. I jumped off the ridge and made my way down a grassy chute, arriving at the bridge where a sign announced that I was at Granite Creek. Clark wrote in his journal entry of September 13, 1805…

"I proceeded on with the partey up the Creek at 2 miles passed Several Springs which I observed the Deer Elk &c. had made roads to, and below one of the Indians had made a whole to bathe, I tasted this water and found it hot & not bad tasted The last in further examonation I found this water nearly boiling hot at the places it Spouted from the rocks I put my finger in the water, at first could not bare it in a Second— as Several roads led from these Springs in different derections, my Guide took a wrong road and took us out of our rout 3 miles through intolerable rout."

I was living the journals, standing about a half mile up the creek from the hot springs, lost among the maze of look-alike hills and on the *"wrong road."* After a short *"3 miles"* of a hike along what was called the Fish Creek Road, I finally reconnected with the well-marked Lewis and Clark National Historic Trail, heading west from the trailhead just north of Highway 12. A well-defined tread led me up a steep slope about three hundred vertical feet to the dividing ridge between Mud Creek and Lolo Creek. There the trail flattened, the easy grade helping to increase my pace and my race with the quickly setting sun. According to the map, I had about three more miles to hike to get to my goal of the West Fork of Lolo

Creek stream crossing. From there I planned to walk the highway back to Lolo Hot Springs where I would meet Judy for a shuttle back to the Howard Creek Trailhead.

The well-worn trail disappeared at the western end of the pool-table-flat ridge. The day was waning and I was getting tired, cold, and hungry. I was becoming lost more often. My hip and knee joints were hurting. I was at "the wall" I hit every time I hiked beyond my usual fifteen-mile limit. My body told me to dive off the ridge to the highway and forget any more Day 3 westward miles. But my mind told me to gut it out and finish the last two miles to the stream crossing, where Judy would hopefully pick up my walkie-talkie signal and save me a three-mile highway backtrack to the Lolo Hot Springs rendezvous spot. I made the decision to keep hiking west.

Around mile eighteen, I noticed huge bear tracks embedded in the soft sandy soil along the ridge, encouraging me to make fast tracks down off the ridge to a logging road. From there I climbed back onto another island ridge and followed the top of the cut slope of the highway. Then I made my way through a wet area of spruce, fir, and larch trees, arriving down at the Lewis and Clark Highway at the east end of a large grassy clearing, across from the creek crossing.

With my walkie-talkie signal too weak to reach Judy around the bends in the narrow canyon, I ended up walking the three extra miles to the resort, making it close to twenty-two miles hiked for the day. Like clockwork, I met Judy as she drove into the parking lot. Then we paid a surprise visit to my "little brother" Carl, who worked weekends managing the pool. Carl was like the son I never had—the kid from a broken home who at age eleven was introduced into my life in 1986 through the Big Brothers and Big Sisters Organization. We did what they asked of us and more. We became friends for life. Checking in with my friend, I shared notes about my Lewis and Clark adventure and heard more about his civilian life after an eight-year tour with the Marine Corps. Then, after announcing that I had to get an early start on the trail in the morning, Judy and I said goodbye and shuttled back to Howard Creek and my truck.

Twelve hours after I had left on the third leg of my journey, I returned to *Travelers' Rest II,* where I readied a lunch, repacked my pack, and set out my clothes for Day 4. Then I read the journals before falling off to sleep, dreaming about Lewis and Clark and me.

Day 4

October 26, 2002

The day was clear and eighteen degrees at *Travelers' Rest II* when I loaded my 10-speed bike in the back of my pickup for the shuttle to Lolo Pass. Heater on high, I made my way west on the highway, driving past the collage of familiar Lewis and Clark scenes of *Woodman Camp*, the Howard Creek Trailhead, *8 PM Camp*, and the phantom Lolo Hot Springs trail section. I pulled into the newly constructed multi-million dollar Lolo Pass Visitor Center and locked my bike to a lamppost, then drove back and parked the Nissan in the pull-out on the north side of the highway, just west of where I ended my trek yesterday. Strapping on my daypack, I darted across the highway and quickly tied in with the trail, making my way to the West Fork of Lolo Creek where I immediately noticed there was no bridge or obvious walking logs to get across the twenty-foot-wide stream. It looked like a soaker in the making. I had been advised to hike from the top of the pass down to the bottom, which made sense because if I fell in the creek I'd have a truck heater to use to dry out and get warm. It was a good ten degrees colder than at the house, perfect conditions for becoming an honorary member of the Polar Bear Club.

I surveyed my options. An ice dam had formed in the backwater and over the top of a half-submerged log about fifty feet downstream, which looked like a sketchy stream crossing. I checked further upstream, bush-whacking my way to another log that spanned the creek. A glossy sheen of ice covered the back of the log that had broken-off sharp staubs sticking out of it like quills on a porcupine's back, which convinced me this "bridge" was definitely not safe enough to use.

With only the two dangerous stream-crossing options, for a brief moment I thought about quitting and giving up on the idea of getting across the creek. But "quit" wasn't in me as I crashed my way back downstream through the undergrowth to the half-submerged-log ice dam. I knew the thin ice that had formed in the backwater on the upstream side of the log wasn't strong enough to hold my weight, but *maybe* the iced-over log dam was.

The icy "bridge" crossing looked like a narrow sheet of greased glass. If that wasn't reason enough to take a rain check on this section of trail, a staub-quilled tree that lay perpendicular over the log "ice-bridge" should have turned me around.

Stubbornly refusing to quit, I inched my way out onto the ice-covered log, my arms stretched out like a tightrope walker, ready to meet my fate. Heel to toe, heel to toe, the log felt stable but definitely not safe, as I slowly approached the six-inch downed tree that lay across the log bridge. Ten feet out I stopped and did a quick reconnaissance. The peaceful sound of gurgling water filled the spruce and fir grove as ice-flattened bubbles slipped beneath my feet. Getting vertigo as I watched the mesmerizing bubbles, I concentrated instead on the spiny-backed tree obstacle in front of me. Locked in the upstream ice, the tree cantilevered at least a foot above the ice-dam bridge, triggering thoughts of turning around before it was too late. But, determined to get to the other side, I erased any midstream turnabout ideas, raised my right boot high over the suspended tree—breaking off a staub in the process—and crunched down on the thickest of the thin ice.

It happened quickly. What I thought was part of the log *wasn't*. My right foot broke through the ice, and my left foot slipped off the edge of the log as I fell knee-deep into the ice-cold water. "Damn!" I yelled out. In survival mode I quickly jumped back on the log bridge. "Damn!" I yelled again as I slipped back into the depths of the pool, feeling the frigid water bite at my skin. Giving up on getting back on the log, I made my way through the backwater, sloshing my way onto the south bank of the creek.

I stood freezing on shore, shaking from the fright of what had just happened and the cold that had started penetrating into my two soaked feet and calves. I needed to make a quick decision to either recross the stream and warm up in my truck or continue to Lewis and Clark's *Glade Creek*

Camp, which was still a good six miles away. Wet, cold, and shivering, I decided to be as true to the *real* 1805 experience as possible and head toward Lolo Pass, drip-drying the freezing lower part of my body in the ten-degree frosty air.

After a fruitless fifteen-minute, teeth-chattering, bone-chilling, toe-tingling, all-out search for the trail, I was thinking I'd made the wrong decision by going up the mountain instead of back down and across the creek to get some heat. But my guilty conscience about cheating with this reenactment journey worked to keep me moving so I wouldn't freeze as my pants were already doing. Finally I located a freshly cut-out path and made my way through the wind-blown timber and leftover logs of a relatively recent logging operation. Trees blazed with historical markers and rock cairns marking the logging road junctions helped guide me as I hiked up the winding path with my feet feeling like they were getting poked by thousands of needles. Two miles short of Wagon Mountain the trail faded and eventually disappeared with no sign of tread, historical markers, or any striped ribbon flagging. Wandering around lost, I eventually found a faint hint of a trail and a shred of flagging. But I was not finding any obvious peeled trees since crossing onto the north-exposed slopes on the south side of Lolo Creek.

The mystery of the lack of Native American peeled trees perplexed me as I repeatedly got lost, then found the trail again and again, heading to the Corps of Discovery's third camp west of Travelers' Rest at Glade Creek. Did the Native Americans use only mature ponderosa pines for food value, or would they have also used the western larches, lodgepole pines, firs, and spruces? The ponderosa pines, which were the dominant species on the south-facing slopes of the canyon, were pretty much missing on the north-facing slopes. If they preferred these trees to the others, that would explain why I wasn't finding any Native-carved trees. But if they used the other tree species as backup food sources, then maybe I just wasn't being observant enough to find them. I kept pondering the question as I continued to search for the trees.

Just below and to the east of Wagon Mountain, I started picking up easy-to-follow tread again with a gentle grade that led me through a mature forest of spruce, fir, and larch trees, bringing me into a sun-filled logging clearcut on the southwest side of the divide. I sat down on a parka-cushioned blackened stump and took off my boots and socks to let the sun warm my feet, looking out at weathered-gray and fire-charred-black tree skeletons that stood like huge scarecrows in the large opening, piercing the fall scene of golden larch-dotted mountainsides. What surprised me was that I was at least five hundred vertical feet higher than Lolo Pass. The non-topographic Forest map made it appear as if I should have been ascending a mountain all the way to the Lochsa River-Lolo Creek divide, not having to hike down to get back up to the pass that lay hidden behind an unnamed mountain about a mile to my west. *Glade Creek Camp* was also tucked in somewhere behind *No-Name Mountain*. It was my goal to find it, to set foot where Lewis and Clark and the Corps of Discovery camped on September 13, 1805.

Thirty minutes later, with my feet warmed up, I put on my still-damp socks and boots, repacked my pack and headed out along the debris-lined trail through the middle of the fairly recent clearcut, descending into the last finger drainage at the head of the West Fork of Lolo Creek.

About a mile from the Wagon Mountain overlook, I got lost again when the narrow path turned into a logging road and the Lewis and Clark Trail historical markers gave out. I had been heading on a southerly course, but now I was traveling due west along a dusty log-hauling road. Off in the distance I could make out a huge rock outcrop that stuck out of the trees like a giant granite thumb pointing to the heavens, which appeared to be northwest of the highway, far from where the trail should have been heading. I turned around and backtracked to the last historical marker-blazed tree. Peering down over the edge of the road, I discovered the log-camouflaged trail disappearing into a thick forest of spruce, fir, and lodgepole pine.

I dropped off the road and descended into the trees, making my way over newly constructed "elevated puncheon" and a log bridge that spanned the last little trickle of Lolo Creek as I crossed the imperceptible Bitterroot Divide into Idaho. Then I followed a series of old logging roads that took me to a lodgepole pine park, where I picked up the path again, leading me past a large sinkhole and dead-ending at the Packer Meadows Road.

Standing on the road, I tried to figure out where the trail went. Facing me was a fairly thick wall of lodgepoles, spruce, and subalpine firs, hiding golden-brown grassy openings that peeked at me from narrow breaks in the trees. I took off my pack and brought out the map, which showed the route of the historic trail heading across the road into the wall of evergreens to the grassy glades. Bringing out the journals, I paged forward to what Clark wrote on September 13, 1805…

"…we proceeded over a mountain to the head of the Creek which we left to our left and at 6 miles from the place I nooned it, we fell on a Small Creek from the left which Passed through open glades Some of which ½ a mile wide, we proceeded down this Creek about 2 miles to where the mountains Closed on either Side crossing the Creek Several times & Encamped."

The *"Small Creek from the left"* had to be Pack Creek, the drainage I was in. To follow where they *"proceeded down this Creek about 2 miles to where the mountains Closed on either Side,"* I broke through the draping arms of subalpine firs, coming out into one of the *"open glades."* Hunting around for the continuation of the recent-made trail tread along the chain of boot-sucking, spongy wet meadows, I came up with nothing except another couple of soaked feet. Squishing my way back to the road, I did a quick search for the trail to the east and soon arrived at Packer Meadows—a favorite spot for the Native Americans to dig for camas roots, and the only glade in the area that was, as Clark referred to it, a *"½ a mile wide."* Striking out on finding any more trail tread, and not wanting to slosh my way through the series of *"open glades"* to the Corps of Discovery's *Glade Creek Camp,* I made my way toward Lolo Pass along the road.

A quarter mile short of the visitor center, at the junction with Forest Road 5670, I took a left and headed south with the hope of finding where the Corps *"Encamped"* on the night of September 13, 1805. I noticed the series of *"open glades"* continuing off to my left, forming a necklace of gently sloping meadows that extended to *"where the mountains Closed on either Side."* Paralleling the glades along the road, and approaching what I guessed was the *"2 miles"* to where Clark stated they *"Encamped,"* I was confronted with an impenetrable wall of trees protecting the identity of the *Glade Creek Camp.* Disappointed to give up on the campsite search, but needing to get the bike shuttle done before black ice formed on the highway, I decided to reverse course and head to the Lolo Pass Visitor Center.

I arrived back at the newly crafted interpretive center where I rested on one of the log benches. A couple of workers assembled another log bench nearby as I ate my lunch and studied the map. From *Glade Creek Camp,* the Corps of Discovery had followed the main ridge between Highway 12 and Pack Creek on the Idaho side of the divide. The *"approximate"* segmented line on the map showed that when they got close to the bottom of the pass, instead of taking the easier route heading west over the Rocky Point ridge, they detoured south, going into some of the steepest, most thickly timbered and brushiest country they would find on their whole journey. The Selway and Lochsa River drainages grew some of the "best" and hardest-to-get-through brush around. I had hiked and crawled through it. I'd cursed it out. But why did they go that way? Was Old Toby actually trying to get them lost, or did he just mistakenly take the more heavily used and obvious *"road"* that the Native Americans in Montana traveled to get to the salmon fishing on the Lochsa River? Clark noted on September 14, 1805…

"we Crossd. Glade Creek above its mouth, at a place the Tushepaws or Flat head Indians have made 2 wears across to Catch Sammon…"

Letting go of what would forever remain an unsolved mystery, I got ready for my steep downhill ride to the bottom of the pass. Soon I was sealed from head to toe with wind pants, parka, wind breaker, wool hat, and thick Hot Finger ski gloves. I unlocked my bike and mentally prepared for the suicide mission I was about to take as the loud air-piercing jackhammering of an eighteen-wheeler's jake brakes announced its descent into Montana. I looked at my wristwatch and read the time. 4:30. A muted gray painted the late autumn sky.

I walked my 10-speed to the starting line at the north end of the large parking lot, stepped over the high bike center bar and said a silent prayer to live beyond the next ten minutes. A quick countdown and I was off, merging onto the newly paved highway. Soon the wind whistled in my ears, the natural speed indicator telling me I was already going too fast for comfort. Fifteen miles per hour…twenty…twenty-five, the wind stream became a scream. Thirty…thirty-five, tears formed, making it nearly impossible to see. I squeezed on my brakes and the worn rubber pads on steel squealed, the bike slowing enough so I could feel in control. A pickup truck veered around me from behind, barely going faster than I was. I loosened my grip on the brakes and played tag with the truck, the wind causing more tears in my eyes and screaming in my ears, my face going numb and my nose and toes feeling a prickling pain in my wet boots. Trees were a blur as the pickup truck acted like a pace car in a race to the bottom of the pass. I flew down the mountain, biking faster than I'd ever skied, faster than any sane person should go on a bike without goggles or a helmet and riding on two bald tires!

I neared *Suicide Corner*, the second tight-turn bend going up Lolo Pass and the site of many crashes over the years. One time I'd seen a motorcyclist lying on the ground, his motorcycle lying on its side next to him, with an emergency medical technician performing CPR. The memory of the up-and-down motions of one person trying to save another was locked deep in my psyche as I closed in on the tight bend in the highway, my right hand working hard on the rear brake, my left hand feathering the front brake, slowing. Then, as if on cue, another loud sputtering of jake brakes split the air from behind me. Thinking about that motorcyclist who died taking the corner too fast, I skidded to a stop at the side of the road on *Suicide Corner*, the tall gray box of a semi trailer flying by me, blowing a cold tunnel of air into my thankfully still-alive body. Before I lost my nerve I took off again, continuing the face-numbing and feet-tingling cold ride the rest of the way to the bottom of the pass, then pedaled the last two-mile straightway section back to my pickup west of the trail junction. Breathing a huge sigh of relief, I loaded up the bike and brought the Nissan to life, doing a U-turn out of the pull-out, heading back for *Travelers' Rest II*.

After a quick stop at Lolo Hot Springs to update Carl about my trek, I continued rolling east. Rounding a bend in the highway by Hungry Creek, I noticed what appeared to be a trail cutting high across the mountain to the east. Pulling onto the logging road where I had lost the trail the second day of my journey, I stopped in front of the locked gate, got out and looked over the cab at the high ridge to the east. Zeroing in, I could definitely tell there was trail tread cutting a steep line high up on the grassy slope.

Excited to connect with the missing Hungry Creek to Grave Creek trail section, I pulled the keys out of the ignition, locked the doors, and headed out without my pack. Jumping the gate, I began hiking up the logging road, searching above where the visible west-side trail dropped into the creek bottom by the hawthorn tree guardian. The blanket of darkness was quickly settling over the land, making it hard to see as I hiked up the draw looking for some sign of the east-side trail that I felt certain dove into the guts of Hungry Creek. I hiked beyond where I had looked on my earlier search for the missing trail, to the junction with another logging road. After a short jog to the east, I noticed a tiny piece of brown-and-orange striped flagging waving in the light up-canyon breeze along a path that led up the hill to the north. Quickly I jogged up the path, following the flags that marked the well-defined tread like a little kid following candy. "Yahoo!" I yelled into the deepening shadows, celebrating my reunion with the Lewis and Clark Trail that had eluded me earlier.

The trail climbed steeply to the ridge, where I glanced back at my little "toy" truck. With no sign of Judy, who I predicted would soon be driving up the highway looking for me, I dropped off the divide and continued heading east. A half mile later the trail dead-ended above a log cabin private residence on the west side of Grave Creek. I stared out over the valley, imagining where it went from here. My instincts told me the Nez Perce and Salish had probably toughed it out and put the trail straight down the steep slope below me and up an even steeper slope on the east side of Grave Creek.

I hurried back to the ridge and immediately caught sight of Judy's red sedan parked next to mine. "Hey, Judy!" I yelled to the miniature figure a half mile away. "Hey, Judy! I'm up here!" I yelled again into the light canyon breeze, doubling my chances of being heard.

"Hey, John!" Judy's voice was carried by the wind to the ridgetop.

"I'll be right there!" I shouted through megaphone-cupped hands, taking off running down the sandy, slippery slope.

Fifteen minutes later I arrived back at Hungry Creek and reunited with my search-and-rescue party of one. After a quick reminder from her that it was getting dark and I should *not* have been on the trail, we left the trailhead, returning home.

October 27–31, 2002

Temperatures took a nose-dive, so I waited at *Travelers' Rest II* for the below zero readings to moderate before heading further into Idaho.

Day 5

November 1, 2002

The temperatures hovered around zero and the skies were clear when I decided to make my move to head deeper into Idaho. Skipping what I heard was the nearly-impossible-to-find *Glade Creek Camp* to *Colt Killed Camp* trail section, I turned my sights instead on the Wendover Ridge to *Snowbank Camp* section. Lewis and Clark were already far down the Columbia River by this date in 1805, shooting rapids as they closed in on their Fort Clatsop wintering grounds just off the Oregon coast. I was still struggling to get through to the Weippe Prairie, where the Corps of Discovery met the Nez Perce, less than halfway through on my journey from Travelers' Rest. There was no more waiting out the weather. I had to get going before the snows locked me out of the high country.

Frosted white caps covered the mountaintops from a "layover-day" snowstorm, which translated into seven inches at Lolo Pass. It was a Christmas card scene, as winter white had replaced fall brown in a simple stroke of nature's artistic brush.

I was searching for the *Glade Creek Camp* that I couldn't find the last day out on the trail. Clark's journal entry clues of the September 13, 1805 campsite location came alive again…

"we proceeded down this Creek about 2 miles to where the mountains Closed on either Side crossing the Creek Several times & Encamped."

The Nissan cut fresh lines through the wintry white landscape as I made my way along the Pack Creek Forest Road 5670. A good quarter mile beyond where I had ended the search less than a week ago, I came upon an interpretive sign. I read that the *Glade Creek Camp* location was somewhere beyond the thick wall of trees that were packed tighter than sardines in a can behind the sign. Instead of crashing through the snow-laden tree branches, I got back in my rig and continued making tire tracks down Pack Creek, looking for a break in the trees.

After about a half mile, and finding some openings through the trees, but getting too far beyond the *"2 miles"* from Packer Meadows with still no sign of their camp, I did a couple of Y-turns and headed back in the direction of the interpretive sign. A little over halfway back, something caught my attention. I let off the gas, slid to a stop, and studied the scene. Clark's journal… *"where the mountains Closed on either Side crossing the Creek Several times & Encamped."*

This was it! Steep mountains on the left and on the right were *"Closed on either Side."* I could finally see what Kevin Foss, from the Powell Ranger District, had described as the camp location… *"The Glade Creek campsite is at an opening in the trees right before Pack Creek drops into the thickly forested canyon to the west."* Kevin was another Lewis and Clark trekker like me. He had followed their route through western Montana and into Idaho. He knew what he was talking about.

I drove into the next pullout, turned off the ignition, and headed down the steep, slippery slope. Climbing over and around logging debris from a recent shelterwood cut, I broke out of the trees and found myself facing the campsite location, which wasn't what I expected. I figured this meadow, which seemed to be the last of the *"open glades"* before the creek dropped steeply off the divide going into Idaho, would have been larger than the half-acre opening I was staring at. But it was next to Pack Creek for a convenient water source, relatively flat, and had plenty of horse feed for a one-night stay. Yes indeed, I could well have been standing a stone's throw away from where the Corps of Discovery set up their tents, lit campfires, and pastured their horses for the night nearly two hundred years ago.*

* In a cooperative agreement reached by Plum Creek Timber Company, the Idaho State Department of Parks and Recreation, and the Idaho Heritage Trust, the area of the *Glade Creek Camp* has been protected for all future generations. In the fall of 2005, after hearing that there was a newly constructed trail to an overlook of the *Glade Creek Camp*, I returned to see how closely that site matched my proposed campsite location. After taking mileages on the road, I discovered the other site was approximately a quarter mile away, and in a slightly higher and larger glade in the chain of meadows stairstepping down Pack Creek. Because of the slight vagueness in Clark's journal description of the *Glade Creek Camp* location, I feel that any one of the relatively dry *"open glades"* within a half mile upstream of my proposed site could have been the Corps of Discovery's camp on the night of September 13, 1805.

The soft snow-muffled bubbling of water flowing under the ice added to the tranquil streamside camp setting. I wanted so much to cross the ice, to step where they *"Encamped."* But with the memory of the other stream crossing fresh in my mind, I played it safe and turned around, heading back up the slippery slope.

Leaving *Glade Creek Camp*, the Corps of Discovery made their way to the top of the ridge to my west. A logging clearcut extended from the road to the ridge, where there wasn't any sign of tread or trail-marking cairns. Clark's log of September 14, 1805 convinced me that abandoning the next trail section was the right decision…

"The Mountains which we passed to day much worst than yesterday the last excessively bad & Thickly Strowed with falling timber & Pine Spruc fur Hackmatak & Tamerack, Steep & Stoney our men and horses much fatigued."

Back on Highway 12 and after a quick stop at the next interpretive sign a few miles west of Lolo Pass, I drove on to Powell to visit with Wilderness Ranger, Kevin Foss.

"Good morning!" I announced as I walked through the front lobby into the ranger station reception room.

"Good morning." The young woman behind the desk returned the greeting. "Can I help you?"

"Yeah. My name's John Crawford. I was wondering if Kevin Foss is in."

"Should be. Let me ring his extension." She punched some buttons on the desk console. "Kevin, there's a Mr. Crawford down here to see you." Some muted words came from the phone. "Okay, I'll let him know." She put down the phone and looked up. "He'll be down in a minute."

"Thanks a lot!"

A couple minutes later I heard footsteps and a young man appeared at the threshold of the entry-way, holding out his hand. "John…I'm Kevin Foss." Our hands met.

"Good to finally meet you after talking on the phone. I was wondering if you'd have a moment to talk a little more about the Lewis and Clark Trail."

"You bet!" he answered with a definite hint of excitement. "Let's go up to my office."

I followed him through the lobby, up the steps and down the hall to his cubicle in the open-format room. We traded notes about Lewis and

Clark, my trek, and about his treks following the Corps of Discovery. I listened to him describe where Clark had waited for Lewis at the Wendover Ridge Rest Site. Then he gave me information on the different camps heading west: *Snowbank Camp, Lonesome Cove, Sinque Hole, Dry Camp, Hungery Creek Camp,* and *Portable Soup Camp.* I learned about access points, and trail and road conditions. I also learned from the clock on the wall that it was getting late. If I was going to make it to at least the Wendover Ridge Rest Site and back to the Lochsa River before dark, I had to stop talking and start walking. I folded up the maps, said goodbye at a break in the conversation, then backtracked through the maze of offices into the reception area.

"Excuse me."

The receptionist looked up. "Yes…"

"How do I get to the Corps of Discovery's *Colt Killed Camp*?" I asked the question I forgot to ask Kevin.

"Just drive over there." She pointed out the window to a large parking area by the Lochsa River, about a hundred yards away. "Their camp was across from the island."

"Can you see the island from here?"

"You're looking at it!"

I pretended I could make out the island of trees which apparently was camouflaged into the steeply sloped forested background. "Sure appreciate the help." I grabbed a couple brochures. "These free?"

"Yes, they are."

"Thanks. See you later."

"Have a good day."

"You too."

I turned and hurried out the two sets of doors, greeting the frosty morning. Clark wrote in his journal on September 14, 1805… *"Encamped opposit a Small Island at the mouth of a branch on the right side of the river which is at this place 80 yards wide, Swift and Stoney."*

I drove to the parking area and checked out *Colt Killed Camp*. The site was pool-table flat, *"opposit a Small Island"* I could easily see now, and the river *"Swift and Stoney."* With time becoming more of a factor, I quickly finished the self-guided tour, snapped a couple of pictures, backed out of the parking area, and headed west. Clark wrote on September 15, 1805…

"We set out early. the morning Cloudy and proceeded on Down the right Side of River over Steep points rockey & buschey as usial for 4 miles to an old Indian fishing place."

Ten minutes later I pulled up to the blocked-off trailhead on the north side of the highway, near the *"old Indian fishing place."* I brought out the trail-worn journal again, referencing Clark…

"here the road leaves the river to the left and assends a mountain winding in every direction to get up the Steep assents & to pass the emence quantity of falling timber which had falling from dift. causes i e. fire & wind and has deprived the Greater part of the Southerley Sides of this mountain of it gren timber, 4 miles up the mountain I found a Spring and halted for the rear to come up and to let our horses rest & feed, about 2 hours the rear of the party came up much fatigued & horses more So, Several horses Sliped and roled down Steep hills which hurt them verry much The one which Carried my desk & Small trunk Turned over & roled down a mountain for 40 yards & lodged against a tree, broke the Desk the horse escaped and appeared but little hurt."

I would be searching for where Clark *"found a Spring and halted for the rear to come up,"* which was the Wendover Ridge Rest Site. Assuming they probably salvaged the trunk, but not the broken desk that *"lodged against a tree,"* I'd keep an eye out for the very *small* needle of oak hardwood in a very *big* stack of fir trees.

A grove of monolith, butt-swelled cedar trees covered the deep, dark flat. I could hear Wendover Creek just off to my east. The pond that Joseph Whitehouse had referred to in his journal lay beyond the creek. I slipped on my pack, made my way around the steel barricade by the Lewis and Clark Trail historical-marker blazed sign, and walked among the cedar giants.

After I hiked along an easy, fairly level grade for the first couple hundred yards, the Lewis & Clark Trail No. 25 steepened and began switchbacking up the mountain. The real Native American salmon-fishing cut-off-path from the main buffalo trail and the 1805 westward Lewis and Clark Trail went straight up the mountain, with *no switchbacks*.

Around mile two, I began to hit snow and soon lost any sign of the recent-made trail. I turned around and followed my boot tracks back to where I discovered my mistake of having gone straight north up the spine of Wendover Ridge instead of taking a left and contouring around to the west. Another half mile and I was lost again when the trail disappeared into a thick stand of small fir trees on the east side of the ridge. Instead of a backtrack, I bushwhacked straight up the snowy slope and met the path again just to the west of the divide between the West Fork of Wendover Creek and Cold Storage Creek.

The challenge of the disappearing trail tread soon turned into a log-hopping obstacle course as well, as the narrow path wound its way along the thickly forested ridgetop, becoming more like what Clark described as… *"the emence quantity of falling timber which had falling from dift. causes i e. fire & wind."* Around mile three I skied off an icy buckskin log and got whacked with a brush whip across my face, making my reenactment hike even more authentic. I felt the welt below my right eye.

The steep three-mile ascent out of the Lochsa canyon was followed by an easy cruise in three inches of slushy snow along the fairly flat Wendover Ridge. Around mile four, the trail veered off the main ridge and entered a finger drainage of Badger Creek. My excitement grew as I realized the remains of Clark's desk had to be close by. But so was the Wendover Ridge Rest Site. According to the diaries, the crash site was before the rest site. I reread the passage…

"4 miles up the mountain I found a Spring and halted for the rear to come up and to let our horses rest & feed, about 2 hours the rear of the party came up much fatigued & horses more So, Several horses Sliped and roled down Steep hills which hurt them verry much The one which Carried my desk & Small trunk Turned over & roled down a mountain for 40 yards & lodged against a tree, broke the Desk."

Clark's description of the horse wreck seemed to be from after the fact, from reports by the group that caught up to Clark at the rest site. But where was the rest site? I figured I was at least *"4 miles"* from the trailhead, and in an area with the best possibilities of finding a spring. But the map showed that I still had a good mile hike to the Wendover Ridge Rest Site. If the map was correct, then I would have to leave the drainage and go up on the ridge to find the rest spot, where chances of finding a spring were slim. Something didn't add up. Maybe Clark's mileages were off. But history proved his dead-reckoning mileage figures were only off about 42 miles overall in the over eight thousand miles that they traveled. I scoped out the slope below me, checking every tree about *"40 yards"* beneath the trail, hoping to get lucky. But I was in a thick, dark forest of mature timber, which meant that even if I could imagine which tree the desk and trunk had *"lodged against,"* I'd have to dig through five inches of snow and then try to scratch into the frozen ground to uncover the remains of Clark's broken desk.

Convinced that evidence of the crash site would be impossible to find, I soon gave up my search and instead concentrated on looking for the spring Clark hinted might have been lower than what the Forest map showed. Every couple hundred feet I stopped and listened for snow-muffled sounds of a trickling spring, but came up with nothing.

The trail climbed steeply out of the thickly treed draw onto a park-like main ridge of ponderosa pine, with plenty of horse feed for a rest stop. Fairly convinced this was the Wendover Ridge Rest Site, I looked around and found a black "5" stenciled onto an old galvanized metal mile-marker sign nailed to a Douglas fir tree just west of the trail. I wiped off a small section of a snow-covered log, sat down and dug into my pack for some lunch, the map, and journals. Eating a granola bar, I went to the dog-eared page in the journal, scrolling down to Clark's rest site description which perfectly matched what I saw… *"from this point I observed a range of high mountains Covered with Snow from S E. to S W with Their top bald or void of timber."* The jagged crest of the Bitterroot Divide formed on the southeast horizon. Grave Peak and surrounding mountains lay across the Lochsa valley to the south. The Selway Crags stood on the distant southwest horizon. With these clues leading me to believe I was definitely at the rest site, my best guess was Clark slightly underestimated the mileage to the spring, which was probably tucked away somewhere below the ridge where I couldn't hear it. The other possibility was the spring Clark referred to might have dried up over the last two hundred years.*

Beyond the relatively open and level rest site the trail quickly steepened and degraded into sections of disappearing tread, thick brush, and tangled webs of downed trees. A good mile short of the Corps of Discovery's *Snowbank Camp*, the eight inches of snow and worsening trail conditions caused my retreat back to the Lochsa.

* Since my reenactment journey I have learned that the spring was located just to the east of Wendover Ridge, near the rest site.

Retracing my steps down Wendover Ridge, I couldn't help but think about the long detour Old Toby had taken the Corps of Discovery on, which had cost them an extra day and Clark's desk. On their return journey from Fort Clatsop in 1806, they did take the easier high-country route, saving them time and much-needed energy to get back to St. Louis. The steep Wendover Ridge climb and the bushwhack from *Glade Creek Camp* to *Colt Killed Camp* convinced me they had taken the wrong route heading west.

The increasingly long tree shadows hurried me along to avoid hiking down into the Lochsa after dark. Constantly I checked my speed going down the steep, snow-filled, trenched-out trail as I slipped and slid my way along the ridge, descending as fast as possible into the deep, dark canyon. Quickly I passed the rest site, the elusive horse crash site, and the lost trail sections, skirting around the log obstacles and getting my face whipped by the brush that was increasingly hard to see.

Two miles short of the trailhead I strapped on my headlamp, pondering what the Corps of Discovery might have used to find their way in the dark. I figured they used candle lanterns. But they also probably arrived at most of their campsites well before dark, something I was never very good at.

I made my final descent into the guts of the Lochsa, hiking through the monolith cedar trees that had stood witness to the passage of the Corps of Discovery in 1805. I could smell the cool, damp forest, and hear the rushing of Wendover Creek getting louder. The distant tree-muffled sound of the Lochsa River joined the chorus.

A final bend on the dark path and a short flat stretch and I was back at the trailhead and my rig. I took off my pack, leaned it against my truck, and located the hidden key. Vehicle lights approaching from the west probed the nighttime sky along the highway. I hid behind the cab as a pickup truck roared by, the night-piercing headlights quickly disappearing around the bend to the east. I unlocked the driver's side door, tossed in my pack and got in. Engine started, heater cranked to high, I turned on the dome light and grabbed the map from my pack, studying my future. The Corps of Discovery's *Snowbank Camp* of September 15, 1805, was my next goal, either by hiking or driving. I would need to get tire chains if I drove, or get my head examined if I rehiked the steep Wendover Ridge

Trail to get there. I made the decision to go to a tire store in Missoula and buy some snow chains. I would continue to head west following the Lewis and Clark Trail by driving the Lolo Motorway that paralleled a good part of the historic tread to the Weippe Prairie, and start camping out, despite the near zero degree temperatures.

With the engine warmed up, I backed onto the highway and headed back east to get some much-needed rest at *Travelers' Rest II*.

At the Wendover Ridge Trailhead along the Lewis and Clark Highway. (TOP) *Recent trail tread heading out of the Lochsa canyon to Wendover Ridge.* (BOTTOM)

Typical brushy section of trail I found along Wendover Ridge (TOP). *Studying the map on my ascent to Wendover Ridge.* (BOTTOM)

Old mile-marker sign at Wendover Ridge Rest Site.

Taking a break at the Wendover Ridge Rest Site. (TOP) *Overlooking the Lochsa River valley from Wendover Ridge.* (BOTTOM)

Near the highest point I hiked to on Wendover Ridge.

"Blowdown" that blocked my attempt to get through to Snowbank Camp.

At Grizzly Bear Saddle, heading toward Snowbank Camp.

My Snowbank Camp II at the Lost Lake Trailhead. (TOP)
Trying to warm up at the campfire at Snowbank Camp II. (BOTTOM)

Getting going after a long, cold night. (TOP)
Eating breakfast at Snowbank Camp II. (BOTTOM)

Deep tire ruts in the snow on the Lolo Motorway heading for Snowbank Camp.

Snowdrifts along the Lolo Motorway near Snowbank Camp II.

At Snowbank Camp interpretive sign, west of the actual campsite. (TOP)
Near the Corps of Discovery's Snowbank Camp. (BOTTOM)

View into the Cayuse Creek-Kelly Creek backcountry north of Snowbank Camp. (TOP)
Along my "cross-country" route, returning to Snowbank Camp II. (BOTTOM)

Skookum Creek Trail. (TOP)
Looking east from the first overlook along the Skookum Creek Trail. (BOTTOM)

Skookum Creek "falls" along rock outcrop. (TOP) *Wolf track found about halfway up the Skookum Creek Trail.* (BOTTOM LEFT) *Lodgepole thicket on a rare flat bench between Lost Creek and Holly Creek.* (BOTTM RIGHT)

The end of the Skookum Creek Trail where it intersects the Lolo Trail. (TOP) Looking southeast down into the Lochsa valley, after climbing the steep Skookum Creek Trail. (BOTTOM LEFT) Open grassy mountainside to the west of the Skookum Creek Trail where I thawed out my feet. (BOTTOM RIGHT)

Looking southwest across the Lochsa valley with the Selway Crags in the upper right of the picture. (TOP) *Ruts I ran in along the Lolo Motorway, attempting to get to the Sinque Hole.* (BOTTOM)

Day 6

November 2, 2002

I spent the morning buying tire chains and groceries, organizing my camping gear, loading my truck with firewood, and trying to convince Judy and myself that driving the Lolo Motorway this time of year with at least eight inches of snow in the high country wasn't one of the craziest ideas I ever had proposed. By 1 p.m. my truck looked like a loaded down Conestoga, heaped with a week's worth of supplies for my attempt to get through to the Weippe Prairie.

The weather was clear and the temperature hovered around zero as I drove west to continue on my quest. I turned up the heater and enjoyed the warmth while I could. My plans were to make it to *Snowbank Camp* before dark and spend the night as close to the Corps of Discovery's fifth camp west of Travelers' Rest as practically possible. Then, if the snow hadn't drifted the road shut, I would go on to find their camp in Moon Creek at *Lonesome Cove*, then make my way to the *Sinque Hole* area for my second night out, doing short day hikes on the trail as I leap-frogged my way west. If I could get that far, I would attempt to drive to *Dry Camp* and beyond. If I couldn't get past the *Sinque Hole* due to deep snow, I would drop down to the Lochsa River via the Saddle Camp Road escape route and cancel plans of making it all the way.

Within an hour of the house, I pulled off the highway just short of the Powell turnoff and started up the Parachute Hill Road. The *CB Channel 19* sign at the bottom of the mountain was code for logging truck traffic. Experience told me that fully loaded log trucks *had* the right of way. I crept up the road, making my way to the official start of the Lolo Motorway Forest Road 500.

My practice of not using four-wheel drive until absolutely necessary had me slipping up the plowed road to a second spur road that branched off to the right, where I stopped and locked in the hubs. Shifting into four-wheel-drive low, I continued my snail's pace with the better traction, but still the thought of meeting a logging truck worried me.

By the Rocky Point Lookout junction I breathed a huge sigh of relief, as it appeared the log truck traffic had been turning off there. The road I was on continued to be plowed, so I didn't chain up as I made my way past the Corps of Discovery's 1806 *13 Mile Camp*. At Grizzly Bear Saddle the plowing service abruptly ended.

Confidence swelled in me as I slid to a stop with thoughts of the unopened bag of tire chains about to give me the added traction I might need to make it up a very steep and narrow Lolo Motorway. Recent chainless tire ruts from other vehicles added to my confidence of getting through to *Snowbank Camp* and beyond, as I thought, *If they can do it, so can I.*

I dumped the chains in the snow and started to sort out the big tangled mess. Ten minutes and ten cold fingers later I finally had them untangled and stretched out directly behind the back tires on the snow-covered road. I backed up the truck a few feet, got out, wrapped the driver's side chains over the tire, and discovered one *very big* problem. The chains were a good five inches too long! Without the hacksaw I should have brought, there was no possibility of fitting them to the tires.

I drove off the chains, threw them back in the bag and contemplated my options. I could return to the house and cut them to the right size. But that would cost me a good weather day at a time of year when there weren't that many left. Or, I could take my chances and attempt to get through to *Snowbank Camp* without chains.

Before I lost my nerve, I threw the useless bag of chains in the back, hopped into the truck, and started the ascent up the mountain to where my heart was taking me.

About a mile out of the saddle I began to sweat when I started hitting alternating patches of ice and drifted snow. But not to be denied, I made my way past the few turnaround spots, extending ever farther out from safety as I slipped up the ruts laid out before me like two long lures enticing me on, keeping precious momentum.

With another big sigh of relief, about four miles short of the Corps of Discovery's *Snowbank Camp* of September 15, 1805, I topped out on a small flat bench along a ridge, pulled into an unimproved campsite next to the *Lost Lakes Trail* sign, and cut the ignition. I cranked down the window, letting in a deep, snow-cushioned hush that backdropped the ringing in my ears. I absorbed the peaceful setting for a few seconds, then stepped out onto the crunchy snow in my soft rubber-coated, felt-lined, below-zero-rated snow boots, feeling a little guilty with the thought of the members of the Corps of Discovery having worn moisture-absorbent deer-hide and buffalo-hide moccasins.

A snow-filled fire ring with conveniently stacked firewood rounds nearby was next to a snow-covered tent flat. I wouldn't tempt fate with driving any further west this late in the day, and would set up my camp here. Soon the pile of gear and split firewood in the back of the pickup became what I called my *Snowbank Camp II*, complete with a three-season Kelty Dome tent, a campfire flinging sparks into the frosty air, and my Pocket Rocket MSR stove on a log round "countertop" chugging away, heating water for Mountain House Turkey Tetrazzini. The Corps of Discovery had a much different meal as Clark described on September 15, 1805…

"Concluded to Camp and make use of the Snow we found on the top to cook the remnt. of our Colt & make our Supe." He also noted… *"From this mountain I could observe high ruged mountains in every direction as far as I could See."*

I wandered up the ridge from camp, and explored what I could while dinner was "cooking". At a break in the trees a stone's throw away from camp, I scanned the view to the north to the *"high ruged mountains."* Williams and Rhodes Peak rose up like a couple of snow-covered seamounts, standing high above the ocean of mountains. Kelly's Finger stood impressive in the background. It was as if I had gone back in time, witnessing what the Corps of Discovery probably saw, discovering these mountains with them.

Steam rose off the log cook bench and lured me back to camp, as a pink afterglow reflected off wispy mares-tail clouds, bathing the snowy landscape. I poured two cups of boiling water into the Mountain House packet, as the dried flakes became a scrumptious-looking concoction of turkey, asparagus, and wine sauce. While I waited for the main course, I drank some hot chocolate and ate cheese and cracker hors d'oeuvres.

A vibration broke the wintertime silence as a four-wheel-drive pickup appeared around the first bend going west from camp. I waved and the two guys inside returned the greeting with this-guy-is-nuts-for-camping-out-in-this-weather looks planted on their faces, their rig quickly disappearing around the first bend heading east toward *13 Mile Camp*.

As darkness descended upon the land, I quickly ate the rehydrated Mountain House cuisine, standing as close to the snapping, crackling, and spark-spitting fire as I could, doing 180s to get my front side warm, then my backside. The Nissan, which I had moved, was smashed into a snowdrift on the opposite side of the road from my campsite, and stood as a tempting alternative to feeling like I was on an expedition in the Antarctic. But my ethics wouldn't allow it. The Lewis and Clark party *didn't* have a rig they could get into to get out of the cold, and they *didn't* have –20-degree-rated sleeping bags, or a pickup filled with split firewood, or ski gloves, wool hats, thermal long underwear, and Mountain House cuisine. The journals came alive again with Clark's description of September 16, 1805…

"I have been wet and as cold in every part as I ever was in my life, indeed I was at one time fearfull my feet would freeze in the thin mockersons which I wore."

Case closed. The keys to the pickup would remain in my pocket. The colder I got, the more authentically my modern day reenactment would mirror what the Corps of Discovery experienced in 1805.

By 7 p.m. my reenactment was getting even more real as I continued to throw more wood on the fire. It was getting damn cold out. But with it still too early to get into the tent, and too late to go on a hike, I continued to watch sparks fly into the night.

Suddenly another vibration broke the wintertime silence as two headlights probed the ridge like a couple of UFOs about to land at my campsite. The full-size pickup slipped and slid its way east, as I waved to the invisible hunters or weekend wanderers in the dark cab. The winter silence quickly replaced the grind of the motor as the truck disappeared around the bend in the road below camp.

By 8 p.m. I traded standing by the fire for going inside the tent and slipping into my five-season *Hollofil II*, super-insulated Slumberjack sleeping bag. Snuggled up in my bed for the night, I read more of the journals and studied the map by battery-operated lantern light. I barely heard the crackling of the dying fire. But what I heard next was a loud and very clear *eerie howling* that came from down off the ridge to the south, sending chills down my spine. I turned off the light and listened. A few last crackles and pops from the fire broke the deep silence. Then I heard the long, drawn out, mournful, eerie howl again. I put away the map and journal, slithered into the depths of my sleeping bag, and zipped myself in for the night, shivering from the cold and the *elusive lone wolf* lurking in the canyon below.

Day 7

November 3, 2002

I woke from a long, nearly sleepless, well-below-zero night—my sleeping bag covered with every article of clothing I could find to ward off the chill that penetrated my thick *Hollofil II* defense. Now I was faced with an even colder proposition...to leave my bag and slip into very cold clothes, which would be like jumping through a hole in an ice-covered mountain lake. I lay there, thinking about leaving the relatively warm insides of my cocoon, and also thinking about my swollen bladder that wouldn't allow me to wait any longer. 5...4...3...2...1...I flew out of the bag and quickly slipped into my stiff, frozen jeans. ***"Brrrrrrrrr!"*** Frosty breaths filled the confines of the tent. Quickly I finished dressing, slipped on my ice-cold boots, and emerged through the small tent flap.

After post-holing through the snow to the "bathroom" in the woods, I hopped around *Snowbank Camp II* like a rabbit in the frozen boots I should have thawed out in my sleeping bag. I was just too cold to deal with starting a fire or lighting the gas stove. A half-dozen jumping jacks didn't change things. I was freezing my butt off!

The sun hid behind the Bitterroot Mountains far to my east. I checked my watch. 6:30. It would be at least another hour until I would feel any solar heat. Everything was crunchy cold and deathly quiet. There wasn't any wind, nothing to break the peaceful silence of the wintry scene.

My fingertips, nose, and toes were starting to go numb. I jumped up and down some more, debating the ethics of using the Nissan's heater to stop feeling like a nearly frozen member of the Lewis and Clark reenactment party of one. Back in February of 1978, on an eight-day snowshoe trip into the depths of the Selway-Bitterroot Wilderness with my friend Don Baty, I would have done nearly anything to have had a heater to warm up by. Four days out in the backcountry at twenty-below-zero temperatures, I had felt even colder than I did now, my sweat freezing every time I took a break from trudging through the snow, and our moisture-producing breaths inside the tent freezing on the ceiling and falling as ice crystals with every little movement. We had to deal with putting on frozen boots each morning and making fires at night that sank from sight into the deep snow. We were constantly melting snow for water simply to survive. Convinced I didn't want any kind of replay of that wilderness snowshoe trip, and throwing out my Lewis and Clark reenactment purist ethics, I went back to the tent, grabbed the maps and journals, then crunched my way over to the truck and easy heat. The engine roared to life and I waited as cold air blasted out into the cab. In five minutes the cold changed to *almost* warm. After ten minutes I started to thaw out, feeling the tingling in my fingers and toes. Gritting my teeth, I read Clark's journal entry for September 16, 1805, the day they had left *Snowbank Camp* heading for *Lonesome Cove*…

"began to Snow about 3 hours before Day and Continud all day the Snow in The morning 4 inches deep on The old Snow, and by night we found it from 6 to 8 Inches deep I walked in front to keep the road and found great dificuelty in keeping it as in maney places the Snow had entirely filled up the track, and obliged me to hunt Several minits for the track."

Patrick Gass wrote in his journal for September 16, 1805…

"Last night about 12 o'clock it began to snow. We renewed our march early, though the morning was very disagreeable, and proceeded over the most terrible mountains I ever beheld. It continued snowing until 3 o'clock P.M. when we halted, took some more soup, and went on till we came to a small stream where we encamped for the night. Here we killed another colt and supped on it. The snow fell so thick, and the day was so dark, that a person could not see to a distance of 200 yards. In the night and during the day the snow fell about 10 inches deep."

William Clark's *"I was at one time fearfull my feet would freeze in the thin mockersons which I wore,"* again made me think about how "authentic" my trek was really becoming. It also made me feel a little guilty for not building a fire to get warm instead of using the truck heater that thankfully had started to bring back feeling to my extremities. But I'd have to conserve my firewood, both for traction and future campfires along the Motorway. I felt the two rigs that drove by yesterday were proof I could possibly make it through the eight to ten inches of snow. The map showed I was close to the 6,890-foot triangulation point at my Lost Lakes Trailhead camp, which was slightly below the highest elevation I would reach on the road to the Weippe Prairie. Assuming the snow depth wouldn't increase much on my way west, I figured the drifted sections would be the only wild cards in my decision to continue heading west with my rig.

After finally thawing out, I turned the engine off and went back out into the frigid alpine air, my curiosity leading me west along the tire ruts on a short reconnaissance to see what the road conditions were like above *Snowbank Camp II*. After initially descending into a shallow saddle, the road contoured around the snowy slope, then became a solid sheet of ice going up a steep grade where I could see my truck *careening* over the edge and *tobogganing* down the mountainside. Convinced I couldn't safely drive any farther west, I dejectedly returned to camp and began dealing with breakfast. I brought the Pocket Rocket stove to life, then jabbed a hole with my knife through the layer of ice in my gallon plastic jug, filling my stainless steel pot with slushy water and placing it on top of the yellow-tipped flames. I felt lost with the knowledge that any more westward travel would have to come to a screeching halt on this snowy ridge, which was still four miles short of my goal of getting to the Corps of Discovery's *Snowbank Camp*. It was all over; my dreams would have to lie fallow for at least another year. I grabbed the pot handle and poured the boiling water into my stainless steel Sierra cup. While I ate my oatmeal I thought about how I could possibly prolong my trek into Idaho. Maybe, as long as I was this far into the high country, I could at least hike to *Snowbank Camp*. I might also be able to access more of the Lewis and Clark Trail west of here by hiking up one of the trails from the Lochsa River. Excited about having some plans for getting a little farther west, I quickly finished breakfast, readied my pack and started hiking in the ruts, heading for the Corps of Discovery's campsite of September 15, 1805.

Within two miles from *Snowbank Camp II*, as I hiked west along the Corps' 1806 eastward route, the ice-covered road turned back to pure snow where I noticed somebody had gotten stuck attempting to get through some deep drifts. Obvious shovel marks cut into the snowdrifts told me that even chains might not have been enough to get me through.

Continuing around a bend in the road I found a Lewis and Clark Trail historical marker tacked to a post, marking the Wendover Ridge Trail's junction with the road, which was about a mile from where I turned around on my climb out of the Lochsa two days earlier. Although the journals indicated the Corps of Discovery continued ascending to "the top" of the mountain, I decided against post-holing into the snow off the road and continued hiking in the tire ruts.

A mile beyond the Wendover Ridge Trail junction and about four miles from my *Snowbank Camp II*, a large brown-stained sign grew out of the eight inches of fluffy snow…

Lewis And Clark Route
"Snowbank Camp"

> *Lewis and Clark ascended the steep mountains from the Lochsa River below to a place a short way above here and camped for the night on September 15, 1805. This site is commonly called "Snowbank Camp".*

The saddle flat I was on wasn't the real *Snowbank Camp*. Their campsite was a *"short way above."* I wandered around, found a cut-off log on the thickly treed flat, brushed off the snow and sat down to study the journals and map. Clark wrote on September 15, 1805, from Wendover Ridge…

"after two hours delay we proceeded on up the mountain Steep & ruged as usial, more timber near the top, when we arrived at the top As we Conceved we could find no water and Concluded to Camp and make use of the Snow we found on the top to cook the remnt. of our Colt & make our Supe."

Patrick Gass added in his journal entry of September 15, 1805…

"We then proceeded on our journey over the mountain to a high point, where, it being dark, we were obliged to encamp. There was here no water; but a bank of snow answered as a substitute; and we supped upon soup."

I looked at the map and confirmed that if I had continued hiking above the Motorway at the trail junction, angling off Wendover Ridge to the northwest, I probably would have found their camp. It looked like my location was about a half mile west of *Snowbank Camp*, along the Corps of

Discovery's route of September 16, 1805, when they were heading from *Snowbank Camp* to their next camp at *Lonesome Cove*. To get to their September 15, 1805 campsite I would have to hike cross-country, heading east out of the saddle.

I repacked, took a mental compass bearing through the trees, and broke trail up the steep, snow-filled slope above the unimproved campsite. Over and around staub-quilled logs I went, traipsing up the mountain, until I arrived at a flat ridge a short half mile out of the saddle. Feeling the excitement of possibly being at their old campsite flat, I pulled out the journals to compare notes with Clark…

"From this mountain I could observe high ruged mountains in every direction as far as I could See."

I was on a thickly forested bench, with nothing like the views William Clark described in his journal. But it was definitely a large enough flat for thirty-three members of the Corps of Discovery, and Old Toby and his son, to have camped. I put away the journal and headed north from the quarter-acre flat, punching through the snow up the moderately sloped ridge, trying to discover where William Clark would have been standing in 1805 to see what he described. At the crest of the ridge I came upon a bluff that overlooked the Cayuse Creek and Kelly Creek backcountry. This had to have been where Clark *"could observe high ruged mountains."* I absorbed the history as I looked out over the vast amphitheater of sparsely treed ridges topped with immense granite spires. Nearly two hundred years separated in time, I was probably standing where William Clark had stood on September 15, 1805, as I looked out at the wilderness that hadn't changed much except for two centuries of forest fire burn mosaics. I stared out at the unclassified wilderness, mesmerized by its beauty, my eyes following the wild ridges and valleys I knew I would return to explore some day. The panorama to the north, though, only half explained Clark's description that he saw *"mountains in every direction."* I took a couple of pictures and left the rock outcrop, in search of the other vista to which Clark might have been referring.

I returned to the quarter-acre tree-sheltered camp flat. Except for the snow, there wasn't any water, just as Clark described on September 15, 1805… *"we could find no water and Concluded to Camp and make use of the*

Snow we found on the top to cook the remnt. of our Colt & make our Supe."

I could *see* the Corps of Discovery now, almost two hundred years later, nearly starving after their torturous climb out of the Lochsa canyon, dining on the remains of the colt. They were cold, wet, tired, and hungry. I felt their presence here more than I had anywhere else. I could feel their pain. I had hiked where they had traveled. I had mushed my way through the same amount of snow. It was even colder now than it had been in 1805.

Further exploration led me to another rock outcrop just to the south of the *Snowbank Camp* flat. Like being in another huge amphitheater, my view opened up to the south to frozen waves of steep ridges and valleys extending across the Lochsa valley to the high, rugged Bitterroot Divide to the southeast and the Selway Crags' crest far off to the southwest. This might have been the other half of the vista Clark had mentioned in his journal.

A stone's throw from where Patrick Gass wrote they *"supped upon soup,"* I sat on the sun-warmed rock outcrop and ate a store-bought hoagie sandwich while I studied my future route on the Clearwater Forest map. I figured the two access roads to the Lolo Motorway west of here would be as steep and slippery as the road I had just driven, which eliminated any more driving ideas. But I noticed a trail going up Skookum Creek farther downriver, a few miles west of where the Corps of Discovery camped on the night of September 17, 1805, at the *Sinque Hole,* that could be my ticket to the high country. I knew the weather wouldn't hold much longer. Skookum Creek would probably have to be the farthest I'd venture west. Giving up on any more cold-weather camping, I'd return to *Travelers' Rest II* and drive to the trailhead early in the morning.

I folded the map and headed east, hiking cross-country until I reconnected with the Motorway, where I alternated between following my old tracks and letting my wandering spirit take me off the road to check out the sun-exposed, snow-melted, steep alpine grassy meadows, as I made my way back to *Snowbank Camp II.* When I returned I efficiently broke camp, loading the leftover split firewood, tent, stove, sleeping bag, and duffle bag of clothes in the back of the pickup. Then I headed down the mountain in four-wheel low, descending into the depths of the Lochsa canyon as the last rays of the setting sun cast orange and pink hues across the undersides of a wave-ribbed cirrus sky.

NOVEMBER 4, 2002

The weather remained clear, with temperatures staying below zero, prompting the decision to lay over a day at *Travelers' Rest II.*

Day 8

November 5, 2002

I wound my way down the Lochsa canyon, traveling the corkscrewing Highway 12 in the darkness for the start of my last day on the trail in Idaho. It was early. Only a handful of logging trucks were out at this time in the morning, and one lone Lewis and Clark trekker heading to the Skookum Creek Trailhead. My plan was to hike up Skookum Creek as fast as possible to get to the Lolo Motorway, then head east along the divide to the *Sinque Hole*. If I kept up a good enough pace, I figured I'd have enough daylight to get to my goal and return to the Lochsa before dark.

I pulled into the closest access point at the Eagle Mountain Trailhead, the early morning cloud-filtered light timing my arrival. Quickly I grabbed my pack from the passenger seat, checked to see if the camera and tape recorder were in my coat pockets, put on my orange hunting vest, and locked the door. Then I walked downriver along the highway until I came to the routed oak sign marking the start of the Skookum Creek Trail.

My fast pace on the moderately steep, narrow path to the prominent ridge that divided Skookum Creek from Lost Creek gave me a quick boost of confidence that I might reach the *Sinque Hole* before my self-imposed 2 p.m. turnaround time. I stopped on the brush-covered ridge and peered down into the canyon at the whitewater rapids of the Lochsa River, flowing in concert with the narrow black ribbon of asphalt that formed the river's north bank. Bright yellow larches stood tall, poking their heads out of the thick carpet of evergreens, dotting the north-facing slopes with their flaming beauty. It was crunchy cold and overcast, an ideal fall day for hiking.

A half mile farther up the trail, the view stopped me again. Like a giant silvery snake, the cascading Skookum Creek wound its way beneath my feet, heading toward the Lochsa River, cutting a demarcation line through the canyon that separated leafless brown-matted brushfields on the east side with a thick evergreen forest to the west. The trail climbed steeply up the canyon paralleling the creek, the next hour of hiking laid out before my eyes.

I scrambled up a large rock outcrop after another half-mile sprint, as the view grabbed my attention again with nature's paintbrush dabbing gray leafless brush on the hillside below me. Isolated twenty-foot-tall Douglas fir trees peeked their evergreen crowns above the alder, false huckleberry, and real huckleberry bushes. Only the sound of a waterfall bridling its way down into the guts of Skookum Creek interrupted the deep autumn silence.

The two-foot-wide tread continued to climb steeply toward the head of the canyon, going into frost-filled, trickling creek draws and out again to brush-covered spur ridges. It was an intimate trail, where I captured the feeling of the creek and the country it cut through. It was a feeling that said, *"Don't hurry…smell the cool, fresh dampness of the decaying leaves, rest amongst the rhythm of the wind-sounding creek, follow the ravens as they play high above the ridges"*. After twenty-nine years of being a fire lookout in some of the most awe-inspiring country around, I had learned how to slow down and be at one with nature. But there was no time to be laid back now. I had to get my rear in gear.

I picked up the pace, quickly leaving the open brushfield, and entered a thick, dark cedar grove along the creek—the dry, dusty trail turning into patches of slushy snow and ice in the shady depths of the canyon. Two cut-out cedar tree downfall were stacked on top of each other on the high side of the narrow path, looking like a headless wooden snowman guarding Skookum Creek where the satiny ribbon cascaded across the trail. Kneeling down, I dipped my cupped hands in the cold crystal-clear water, getting a drink as the flute-like notes of a water ouzel blended with the music of the peacefully flowing stream. This was the place where a person would want to sit back and cool off on a hot August afternoon. On this very crisp, cold day in November, it was no place to stay for long as the bite of winter was already finding its way to my sweaty skin. I finished an energy snack and hopped over the creek, melting into a grove of huge cedar statues lining the path.

I continued my climb on the west side of the creek under the umbrella of the butt-swelled cedar trees, pondering my obsession with putting one foot in front of the other tens of thousands of times to get to a vista, a hidden waterfall, a cedar grove, and a campsite at the end of the day. It was something I loved to do *because* of its simplicity, which allowed me time to think, to contemplate life, to write the chapters in my mind that I could share with others. I had hiked the drumlins, eskers, and glacial moraines of Wisconsin; the birch forests, poplar groves, and deeply eroded waterfall-filled canyons of northeast Minnesota's Lake Superior shoreline; the wilds of the Colorado and Montana Rockies; the Seven Devils Mountains of Idaho; and a good part of the Selway-Bitterroot Wilderness. My footprints and snowshoe tracks reached almost every ridgetop, valley, and mountainside I could see from my summer fire lookout home. Trails were like lures to me, the narrow brown ribbons leading into new, unexplored-by-me country. It was my spirit of adventure that drove my desire to see what was over the next ridge, and what I felt I had in common with Lewis and Clark and the Corps of Discovery.

My decision to hike in my leather boots, which was a good idea in the drier lower part of the canyon, became a big problem as I climbed into steadily deepening wet snow that my boots soaked up like a couple of sponges. My toes were starting to boycott my choice of boots, getting that *tingling* feeling before reaching the *going-numb* stage. I hoped for a break in the clouds and an opening in the trees, for the sun to make an appearance to counter the effect of the chilling snow.

Clark's words of September 16 came alive again…

"I have been wet and as cold in every part as I ever was in my life, indeed I was at one time fearfull my feet would freeze in the thin mockersons which I wore."

Wolf tracks in the snow near the head of Skookum Creek looked fresh and were going my way. Fresh elk tracks in a clearing along the trail explained the wolf tracks, and let me know that if I were a hunter I wouldn't go hungry. At their camp at the *Sinque Hole* on the morning of September 18, 1805, Clark explained… *"I proceded on in advance with Six hunters to try and find deer or Something to kill."* He wrote this when they were at the point of near starvation, with the Corps of Discovery having to kill off their colts simply to survive, as he described in his previous day's journal entry… *"a coalt being the most useless part of our Stock he fell prey to our appetites."* At day's end on September 18, 1805, Lewis reported… *"we dined & suped on a skant proportion of portable soupe, a few canesters of which, a little bears oil and about 20 lbs. of candles form our stock of provision."* William Clark and the six men would make a painfully long, thirty-two mile march in a desperate search for game, coming up empty-handed by the time they got into the depths of the drainage that was so appropriately named Hungery Creek. Clark's nightly report on September 18, 1805 reflects… *"made 32 miles and Encamped on a bold running Creek passing to the left which I call Hungery Creek as at that place we had nothing to eate."*

Six miles out of the bottom of the Lochsa canyon, I arrived at the top of the Skookum Creek divide that formed a giant wedge splitting Holly Creek from Lost Creek. There the mountain flattened, the bench covered with dead and dying lodgepole pine trees. Old beargrass stalks poked through the snow under the bare-needled pines, the small brown round seedpods of the once beautiful cream-colored flowers looking like thousands of tiny ornaments on hundreds of Charlie Brown Christmas trees. The seven inches of snow had slowed me down, keeping my feet soaked and tingling cold.

Eating snacks on the run, I continued my snowy march through the lodgepoles, post-holing to the end of the rare mountain flat, slipping up the last steep ascent to the Motorway. With every step my feet were getting colder, the tingling feeling being replaced with no feeling at all. The candy bars, cheese, and crackers weren't countering the chilling effects of the snow and the cold as I approached seven thousand feet in elevation. I made slow but steady progress up to the ridge, troubled by the decision I had to make to return to the Lochsa or risk frostbitten feet. But when the going got tough, the Corps of Discovery *didn't* have the luxury of abandoning their journey and dropping into the canyon bottom where they could simply drive home. Clark's *"fearfull my feet would freeze"* journal quote pushed me up the mountain, guilt-tripping me into toughing it out like they had. They had absolutely no choice but to keep going…cold, wet, tired, and starving, every excruciatingly tough step of the way.

The last trail stretch seemed to go on forever with my two feet starting to feel like a couple of stumps, as I trudged over a series of false summits, each one giving me false hope that I was finally coming to the end of my tough climb out of the bottom of the deep canyon that lay well over four thousand vertical feet below. A brief opening in the clouds created a sun-dappled effect on the alpine meadow cirque just off to my west, teasing me up the steep mountain to get to the place where I could warm up my feet.

Like a mirage, a two-post sign suddenly mushroomed out of the snow, marking the end of the Skookum Creek Trail and my reunion with the Lewis and Clark National Historic Trail and the Native American paths that it followed. Without hesitation I quickly made my way west and dropped into the clearing I had seen from the trail. Sitting down on a large rock near the top of the south-exposed, patchy snow-covered cirque basin, I took off my boots and massaged my feet in the sun that spotlit the meadowy hillside through another opening in the cloud-riddled sky. I peered across the Lochsa valley, making out Chimney Peak and Fenn Mountain that stood as exclamation points on the crest of the Selway Crags divide. I had summited Fenn Mountain twice on backpack trips with my Coolwater Lookout neighbors, Tom and Betsy. My failed, more technical, attempt at climbing Chimney Peak would bring me back to try again some day. The rest of the peaks, knife-edge ridges, valleys, and cirque basins of the Selway Crags had my footprints all over them after nearly three decades of hiking that remote backcountry. I glanced at my watch. 1:30 p.m. It was thirty minutes until my self-imposed turn-around time. The book ***Into Thin Air*** came to mind, in which eight climbers on Mount Everest had lost their lives because they did not turn around from their summit attempts on time. I could see the title to the new book about the fool who didn't follow the rules of the mountains—***Into Thick Brush***. I didn't have any overnight gear.

The painful tingling feeling in my toes told me I wouldn't lose them to frostbite. The map told me that I wouldn't make it to the *Sinque Hole* in the time I had allotted for the remaining eight-mile round trip. The math just didn't add up. Disappointed, I slipped on my soaked boots and made my way back to the trail sign, thinking about adding another couple hours to my turnaround time. Then I thought about fighting that jungle of brush in the lower end of Skookum Creek, after doing an eight-mile jog in eight inches of snow with wet and cold feet. With an obsession like the Everest climbers, I threw caution to the wind, dropped my pack at the foot of the sign and took off with a burst of speed down the conveniently placed ruts in the snow, heading for the *Sinque Hole*.

Two miles later I skidded to a halt between two thick curtains of lodgepoles, my heart pounding out notes to the 1812 Overture. I bent over with my hands on my knees and rested as frosty breaths puffed out of my mouth like an old steam locomotive chugging up a hill. I checked my watch. 2:28 p.m. With the encouragingly fast pace, I started running east again.

At a rare opening in the lodgepole tree tunnel, I made another stop as more vaporous breaths puffed out into the cold alpine air. I panned around, and looked at the tree-framed views into the wild, remote Weitas Creek drainage to the north, then to a rounded-top mountain at the head of Lost Creek off to my east. Hidden from view was Indian Grave Peak, the mountain that stood as a monument to the Nez Perce boy who was buried nearby. The *Sinque Hole* lay further away, a good mile off the mountain's northeast flank. One and a half miles short of my goal I had to swallow a hard pill, knowing I would have to turn around and head home.

Back at the trail sign I strapped on my daypack and dove off the divide, descending toward the Lochsa River. A short way down off the ridge, I slid to an abrupt halt and looked back at the mountain meadow cirque where I had thawed my feet, knowing that it would be the farthest west I would get on my Lewis and Clark trek. It was a hard decision to make, but the drifted snow on the divide convinced me I could go no further.

"Hey, Lewis!" I yelled through the trees, the words floating up to the ridgetop. "Hey, Clark!" I shouted again to connect with the past. Only a deep, total, late-fall silence blanketed the ridge. I wouldn't get a response; the echoes of yesterday had been swept away with the westward breezes of long ago.

Sadly I turned around and continued to retrace my tracks back down into the Lochsa.

Day 9

November 6, 2002

The reason for going cross-country, climbing the steep eastern slope out of Clark Creek on the Montana side of the Bitterroot Divide was to try and locate the *Woodman Meadows* to Grave Creek section of the historic trail. My plans were to hike from west to east in the missing trail section, ending my journey where the Corps of Discovery had begun their tough trip through the Bitterroots on their second day out from Travelers' Rest on September 12, 1805. The conclusion of my Lewis and Clark trek would be at the heart of the valley Judy and I called home.

I topped out on a fairly flat ridge above Highway 12, found a knee-high stump from an old logging operation, sat down and brought out the map. It was a perfect crisp and clear day for hiking, with most of the snow melted in the lower elevations.

The map showed the Lewis and Clark Trail's location to be about a mile north of the highway, which was a good half mile from my location. But I had never heard of anybody actually finding the trail east of Grave Creek where it crossed private property and Plum Creek Timber Company land. The Grave Creek to Clark Creek section was essentially sealed off by private property on the western end. But was there any flagging or recent tread identifying the Lewis and Clark Trail on the Plum Creek land, as the Forest Service had done on their land? The mystery of the trail location, with only the *"approximate"* notation on the map showing me the way, followed me as I started searching for the historic path, heading north along the gentle grass-covered ridge, quickly losing sight of the highway.

Part of the reason I enjoyed western history so much was because of its relatively recent aura. Old abandoned trapper cabins, homesteads, one-room schoolhouses, and mine buildings still covered the west like one giant outdoor museum exhibit, giving me clues about who came before me. But now I was digging deeper into the past, before the time of the old gray-weathered buildings I found on my explorations of the west. I was looking for evidence of a trail that was thousands of years old. To solve the mystery of its location, I knew I would have to use the clues left by the Native Americans who passed this way. I tied into a logging road, and headed northeast toward the main divide between Clark Creek and Potato Gulch.

I stopped at a wide bend in the road, feeling like I was on an island surrounded by a sea of light-tan knapweed stalks that shivered in the wind. Charred remains of an old logging slash pile lay at the base of the fill slope on the low side of the road. I did a scan of the country and noticed a fairly prominent mountain across Potato Gulch to the northeast that dove into a flat ridge, forming a distinctive notch at its base. It looked like a perfect "saddle" for the trail to go through if I was going to put one there. Another mountain rose sharply above me. If my gut feeling was correct, it might put me in the area of the trail where Native Americans traveled to hunt bison in the high plains of Montana and Wyoming, and catch salmon in Idaho, Oregon, and Washington.

My eyes were magically drawn to a broken-topped, old gray-weathered dead tree below me. With the tree guarded by a thick layer of fir boughs and brush, I could just barely make out the classic triangular-shaped scar at its base. A bald eagle, as if on cue, soared above the ridge, cutting graceful arcs across the pale blue sky.

With excitement bubbling over, I ran down the fill slope and quickly made my way to the old tree. Like a ghostly image, the arrowhead-like scalloped edges suddenly appeared from the very old peeled marks in the bark. With a feather light touch, I felt the weatherworn smooth edges, absorbing the Native American energy into my soul. Then, with a feeling of disbelief, I realized I was standing right next to the brush-and-knapweed-camouflaged trench of the historic trail.

Like taking pictures of a newborn baby, I clicked off enough shots of my incredible discovery to fill a small photo album. Then I strapped on my pack and followed the old trench into the woods, crashing through the ninebark, Juneberry, and fir-branch whips for a couple hundred feet before I came upon recent trail tread crossing the ancient Native *"road"*. Solid yellow ribbons, along with orange-and-white striped ribbons, hanging from young fir trees confirmed somebody else had also found the trail. I stepped out of the brush-choked Native path and followed the flag line of the "new" trail, holding my arms out in front of me like I was sleepwalking, spreading the thicket of brush and tree branches as I descended into the gulch to the east. Slowly I made my way along a snow-and-ice-filled tread that alternated with a dry-leaf-and-needle-littered trail bed. Then the flagging disappeared. Momentarily I felt lost without the little ribbons through the tunnel of trees. But the tread kept going, so I continued making tracks on a potpourri of trail sections, some of which were open and easy for hiking and others as thick as a jungle.

I arrived at a narrow thread of a creek that flowed through a grassy flat at the bottom of Potato Gulch, on course for the toe-of-the-slope ridgetop that lay hidden to the east. I stood and felt the peace of the lazy stream, wondering if the Corps of Discovery had stopped at this special spot for a drink or to water their horses. A short hop over the creek, and I cut through the sedge grass and soon came to an old logging road. I hunted for flags, but found none, so I just continued hiking up the path on the opposite side of the road.

The trail led to another old logging road, where again I went in the direction of my best guess, taking a right. I followed a narrow deer path down the middle of the grassed-over old road until I came to another path that branched off to my right through a thick Douglas fir forest. I flipped another coin in my mind and stayed left, following the roadcut which led to yet another fork. Feeling lost and confused in the maze of old logging roads, I scanned the thick, emerald forest for some clue of where to go. A small weather-faded yellow rectangular sign nailed to a tree caught my eye. I walked over to it, making out an *S*, then an *H*, followed by an *O*. I finished the letter game and came up with *NO SHOOTING*, giving me the clue I was at a private-property boundary. I pulled out the map and verified I was on the boundary between Plum Creek Timber Company land and somebody's private property. Putting the map away, I veered north, trying to skirt around the unknown property owner's land.

A few hundred yards away from the *NO SHOOTING* sign I discovered a trail contouring back to the east and took it, soon realizing I was on another braid of the Native path that paralleled the main trench to the south. It was a pattern I had seen before, especially in the trail section west of Howard Creek. Clark wrote on September 12, 1805…

"The road through this hilley Countrey is verry bad passing over hills & thro' Steep hollows, over falling timber &c. &c. continued on & passed Some most intolerable road on the Sides of the Steep Stoney mountains, which might be avoided by keeping up the Creek which is thickly covered with under groth & falling timber."

The trail "braids" were probably made by the Native Americans to avoid the windfall, root wads, and slides. If a log had fallen across the main trail, they probably established a braid until that path also became blocked, requiring them to move again. When the original trail's log obstruction rotted away, they most likely returned to the main trench. Even though I was off the "main" trail, I was still on a north braid of it. If I had swung south, I'm sure I would have picked up other braids paralleling what I now believed was a common-denominator Native-made thread through the land*.

I made my way over the ridge between an unnamed gulch and Potato Gulch, hiking through the notch I had set my mental compass on earlier, adding more credibility to my toe-of-the-slope trail placement theory. Slipping down an icy and snow-covered recent tread on the east side of the divide, I soon lost the trail again where it faded into a brush-choked and downfall-laced hillside. Then it became a game of crashing through the thick brush and young tree branch whips, and climbing over the downfall until I could again locate some flagging, a peeled tree, or a braid of the historic trail trench or tread of the recent trail, leading me through *No Name Gulch*.

Sheldon Creek was a hidden jewel of a stream, a trickling silvery thread of miniature waterfalls dropping into small pools as it wound its way south toward Lolo Creek. A better watering spot than Potato Gulch, perhaps the Corps of Discovery had stopped here for a rest and to water their horses from the two-foot-wide bubbling brook. Clark made reference to the tributaries of Lolo Creek on September 12, 1805…

"at 2 miles assended a high hill & proceeded through a hilley and thickly timbered Countrey for 9 miles & on the Right of the Creek, passing Several branches from the right of fine clear water…"

Intermittent tread continued east of Sheldon Creek, as I followed a

* After my reenactment journey I learned that the Native Americans, on occasion, would travel spread out across the mountains, which would also have created trail braids.

hodgepodge of relatively recent-built trail mixed in with original braids. Just west of the Sheldon Creek-Smith Creek divide I started picking up new fluorescent green and old faded orange-and-white striped ribbons hanging from Douglas firs like Christmas tree decorations, guiding me to the ridge. I made my way through the small trees in a ten- or fifteen-year-old logging unit and arrived at a vista overlooking Smith Creek.

I sat down on a stump at the north end of the ridge and studied the area. Off to my east I could see a toe-of-the-slope prominent notch in the ridge. My instincts told me the trail probably went through the notch, which looked to be a good hour hike away. My goal of getting to Bear Creek, which was probably another half hour hike beyond that ridge, would have to wait until tomorrow when I planned on making it to *Woodman Meadows*, where my Lewis and Clark journey would come to an end. After finishing my lunch, I dropped off the divide, backtracking to my truck, following the flag line and visible tread back to the west.

Finding the trail, difficult in the light of day, became even more challenging in the dusty gray of early evening, as I could barely see my boot tracks in the occasional patches of snow that helped guide me back to where the day's journey began. Descending into Sheldon Creek, I stumbled over downfall, slipped and slid on the snow and ice, and continued to get clawed by the tree branches and brush whips that spider-webbed the trail.

Reaching into my pocket for my knife to cut out a sliver I got from a broken branch staub, I discovered that it was missing. Backtracking my thoughts to where I had it last, I realized I had left it where I'd taken a self-timed posed picture at the peeled tree on the west side of Potato Gulch. After using the tip of the knife blade to trigger the self-timer button, I had jabbed it into a stump and forgotten about it. I picked up my pace in the steadily dropping curtain of darkness, on a course to return to the carved tree.

I jumped across Sheldon Creek and began my ascent out of the valley, using my trail-finding instinct, the barely visible peeled trees, and hours-old boot tracks in the snow to follow the maze of braids of the Native path and recent-made tread through *No Name Gulch* and Potato Gulch.

Like a blind man I reached through the shadow of darkness that had almost completely covered the land, my fingers feeling the rough edge of the stump I thought I had used for a camera base earlier in the day. I started to second-guess my decision to search for the knife, thinking about how at almost every place I went that held special meaning, I tended to unconsciously leave things. Weeks later I usually would get them sent back to me in the mail. Other times they were just lost forever. I felt a connection with this spot, the history coming alive as I could *see* the Native Americans traveling through on their way to the buffalo grounds in Montana and Wyoming and the salmon fishing in Idaho, Oregon, and Washington, and the Corps of Discovery following in their tracks to get to the Pacific and back to Saint Louis. Forgetting the knife was just my subconscious mind wanting to leave something at this very special spot. But my guilty conscience reminded me of my ethics about littering as I began to feel other stumps, searching for the missing knife.

It was just too dark to continue my habit of not using any artificial light to ruin my natural night vision, so I switched on the headlamp that quickly exposed the shiny metal sticking out of the side of a stump about thirty feet below the road. I hurried over and pulled the knife out of the wood, wiped the blade on my pant leg, and dealt with the sliver. After successful finger surgery I made tracks back to my pack at the road cut.

After a quick change into some warmer clothes to ward off the chill of the night, I followed the headlamp's tunnel of light, retracing my route from earlier in the day, arriving at a tempting but dangerously steep old logging skid trail branching off the road to the west and diving into Clark Creek. Taking it would save a couple miles of hiking on the main logging road. So before I could second-guess my decision to chance it, I jumped off the lip of the road and flew down the steep mountainside, my headlamp spotlighting tree and brush whips that flashed out of the night. Slipping, sliding, and hooting and hollering like a kid on some Western Montana Fair ride, I careened down the mountain, skidding to a perfect two-point landing on the valley floor at the road, feeling like an expert boot skier who'd just finished a double-diamond ski run. Following the peaceful trickling of Clark Creek, I hiked the last easy quarter mile back to the truck parked behind the locked gate.

I stared up at the steep, shadowy slope looming above me that I had climbed earlier in the day, listening to Lolo Creek serenade the valley. I imagined being back on that ridge, touching the weatherworn-smooth scalloped edges of the peeled tree, and absorbing the feeling that seemed to touch to the depths of my soul.

Day 10

November 7, 2002

It was another clear, brisk morning when I headed out to connect the Sheldon Creek-Smith Creek divide with the *Woodman Meadows* overlook. Shortly after 8 a.m. I turned off the highway and drove up the Bear Creek Forest Road, searching for signs of the timeworn Native American path. I took a left at a "Y" in the road and soon noticed a tiny piece of faded ribbon hanging from a small fir tree in a grassy opening. Immediately I pulled over, hopped out of the truck and ran up the hill to check it out. "Yahoo!" I yelled out, excited at finding what indeed was a faded version of the same type of flagging I had followed yesterday.

I ran back to the truck, put on my pack, and checked to make sure I had my camera and microcassette tape recorder for trail notes. Then I secured the bear spray to my belt and headed out, hiking up the logging skid trail that lay just to the south of the ribbon marker. As I climbed out of the west side of Bear Creek, I immediately ran into the same thick brush, disappearing tread, and hard-to-find-flagging problems that had plagued me so many times before. But with the main divide in plain sight, it took only a half hour to get to the top, despite the impediments.

I added another name to the maze of unnamed geographical features, dubbing my location as *Target Shooting Ridge*. Paper targets, stapled to trees and posts, were pockmarked with bullet holes. A recently used fire pit sat to the south of the targets, where people could warm up, then plink at the paper bulls-eyes that seemed as if they were staring at me. A quick survey to the west of the roadcut showed obvious tread heading down an old skid trail, so I dropped off the ridge and followed it.

At the bottom of the Smith Creek drainage I got lost again, where the flag line and tread disappeared in the grass and sparsely tree-covered gentle slope of an old logging unit. I wandered the broad, hidden valley, and began my search for clues that would reconnect me with the trail.

Like an old friend, a peeled tree suddenly appeared from across the clearing. Drawn to it, I walked up and was about ready to touch it, when a little voice in my head said, *Look, John, but do not touch!* Listening to my conscience, I stood back and simply stared at the old peeled marks, feeling in an instant the thousands of years of Native Americans who had passed this way. I noticed the teepee-shaped carved opening at the base of the tree was charred black like most of the other Native-peeled trees I had found along the trail. I guessed that to be from the sap that was exposed from the cut, which would have been easily ignited in the huge fire that roared through here on August 20 and 21, 1910, when over three million acres of north Idaho and northwestern Montana burned. Tall gray snags still dotted the landscape, standing like weatherworn memorials after nearly one hundred years of nature trying to lay them to rest. The carved tree put me back on course, as I started to pick up flagging and recent tread again on my way to the toe-of-the-slope pass that acted like a compass guiding me toward the next prominent ridge.

After an hour hike out of the bottom of Smith Creek, I arrived back at the Sheldon Creek divide in the familiar cutting unit where I had turned around yesterday. Across the Lolo canyon to the south more recent evidence of logging showed, with Lolo Peak and its companion Bitterroot Mountain peaks standing tall above it all. With little time for relaxing, I touched the lone flag that marked the divide and quickly reversed my course to Bear Creek.

Back at the truck, I checked out the afternoon route to *Woodman Meadows*, soon realizing I'd brought the wrong map. The Clearwater Forest map that I had didn't show the country east of Camp Creek, where the Lolo Trail Ranch land was located. Without knowing where their property line was, I wasn't sure if I could get through to the *Woodman Meadows* overlook, where I had planned to end my trek. Undaunted, I repacked my pack and headed into the brush opposite my pickup, following old faded ribbons into the bottom of the Bear Creek valley.

The gurgling of the water flowing under a thin membrane of ice was the only sound I heard after crashing through thick foliage to get to the edge of the ten-foot-wide stream. I stood enchanted by the peaceful setting for a minute, then did a fruitless survey for any logs to cross. My only choice, I found, was to walk over a conveniently placed tangled web of leaning-over river birch limbs and brush that would distribute my weight on the ice. Slowly I inched my way out onto the branches, my arms sticking out at my sides like a couple of Cessna wings, trying to keep from being drenched by the creek. Softly I stepped, crunching down on the pliable branches that acted like long skinny snowshoes on the icy surface. Step by careful step I made my way across, feeling the cracking of the thin ice from my weight.

Relieved to make it across, I broke my way through a small opening in the tight brush on the opposite side and entered a deep, dark spruce forest. Finding no sign of the trail, I started to climb out of the mature timber and bushwhacked my way up the slope, heading east. Soon I came upon a very faint recent trail that was marked with a nearly camouflaged, tiny piece of ribbon fluttering from a spindly fir branch in the up-canyon breeze. I made my way up to it, spreading brush as I went. At the base of the tree I stepped into the deeper main Native trail trench that fused with the modern-day tread. From there I crashed through the thickest brush and small trees I had found yet on the trail. For a couple hundred yards I got shredded; then, like magic, the trail suddenly became clear of any more obstacles as new ribbons appeared, waving from tree branches like a bunch of little Fourth of July flags lining a parade route. I hiked through the tunnel of trees, following the flag line up the steep slope to another roadcut at the top of an old logging unit on the Camp Creek side of the divide.

Combing the ridgetop for more flagging, I finally discovered some on a tree that jogged the trail farther south than I thought it would. But my private-property detour yesterday had pretty much confirmed that the Native American trails braided over a fairly wide area. Whoever had marked the route through here, I suspected, had probably just flagged one of the more southerly braids. The flag line brought me past a couple more peeled tree signatures, leading me into the bottom of the old logging unit, where I dropped into a cathedral of mature spruce trees that towered above Camp Creek.

It was another good watering hole where the Corps of Discovery might have taken the time to rest amid the beauty of the tranquil stream. Ice-veneered, the silvery thread peacefully cut its way through the little valley tucked away from the rest of the world. Hypnotized by its subtle beauty, I watched flattened bubbles press up against the bottom of the thin ice, racing for an opening in the glassy surface. I helped them out, shattering the fragile membrane of ice with the heel of my boot, giving the bubbles an escape hatch and me a chance to taste "nature's martini". I reached down with cupped hands, ladled some crystal clear cold water up to my mouth, and drank. Then I dipped again, taking my chances with getting giardia. I brought out my lunch, as my communion with the creek lasted a little longer.

At the top of the next ridge I knew I was getting close to the overlook and the end of my journey. I wanted to slow down, to touch, smell, and feel everything the trail had to offer. But from the position of the cloud-filtered sun I could tell I needed to speed up to make sure I got back to Bear Creek before dark.

I followed a well-defined trail into another no-name gulch, passing a large ponderosa pine peeled tree that confirmed I was on the right path. This was it. There were no more tomorrows in this Lewis and Clark adventure of mine. In a good mile I would arrive above the cattle pasture where my reenactment journey would be over.

At the bottom of *No Name Gulch* I came to signs of civilization—a stock tank, fencing, recent tire tracks on another old unimproved road. I could definitely tell I was getting close to the private property line that would stop my trek dead in its tracks. The tread continued east on the opposite side of the road and I followed it, hiking up an old skid trail, making my way toward the ridgetop.

It appeared to me like a bad dream: a wire fence with a little red sign on a fence post that read *No Hunting, No Fishing, No Trespassing*. My trip was over and I knew it. I couldn't in clear conscience trespass, even if it meant I'd be stopped teasingly short of my goal. Discouraged, I took off my pack and brought out my map. Immediately my eyes focused on two other missing trail sections I hadn't hiked yet. One was the Lolo Hot Springs section. The other was the Grave Creek to Clark Creek section. There also was the Fort Fizzle section further to the east, the location of which I was still debating. I had three days of vacation left, and three more hikes. I would use the last of the good fall weather hiking days to trek through the weekend. The *Woodman Meadows* section would have to wait until I got permission from the ranch for the last day on the trail.

Excited to have plans of postponing the end, I started backtracking with a renewed stride, following the narrow ribbon of a trail and the flags dangling from the trees as the light of day was slowly erased by the steadily increasing shadow over the land. At the pass going into Bear Creek, I came to a road where I lost the trail again and was quickly losing daylight to find it. Being a tortoise on the trail had cost me.

I always had difficulty with admitting I was lost. I had been in the remote Selway Crags when the thickest gray blankets of fog camouflaged the gray talus slopes, and I didn't feel really disoriented until I almost ended up hiking over a cliff I *didn't* know was there. Then there was the time when my friend Gary Winek and I were canoeing in the Boundary Waters of Minnesota and *none* of the small islands in the large Seagull Lake matched with those on the map. But now, without any sign of the trail diving into Bear Creek, I had to admit I was "at least" temporarily *lost!*

Instinct told me to locate *Target Shooting Ridge* and aim for it. But everywhere I looked appeared to be an impenetrable jungle of brush and small trees. A short search, though, led me to the smallest of openings through the thick trees, which I took, spreading brush and fir branches as I dropped off the divide.

In a couple hundred feet my nylon jacket needed some duct tape patches and I needed my head examined for going cross-country instead of taking the logging road. My bearings were off, my trusty "inner compass" no longer guiding me out of this mess. I absolutely didn't want to have to climb back through the brush-and-tree thicket to the road, so I kept wandering through different brush, descending into the depths of Bear Creek.

"Hey, Old Toby!" I yelled into the dusk-filtered canyon from a rare opening in the thick vegetation. "Where am I?" The shout echoed across the landscape, as I hoped in some way the spirit of the long-deceased Shoshone guide could answer my cry for help. I listened closely, but could only pick up a slight whisper of the wind and the breeze-blending rush of Bear Creek.

Soon I arrived at a logging road, guessed left, and started hiking a couple hundred yards upslope and parallel to the creek. Going through a logged area, I kept an eye out for any possible stream crossings.

Things went from bad to worse when the road ended and I had no clue where I was, other than somewhere east of Bear Creek. But I couldn't tell how far up the creek drainage I was. *Nothing* looked familiar anymore. If I bailed off the hill now, I could be faced with another bad stream crossing. But following the path I saw leading into the woods might take me far enough downstream to find a log bridge. I opted for the trail route and took it, disappearing into the deep, dark forest.

Within a couple minutes the initially descending trail started ascending in the direction I didn't want to go, so I returned to the road and bailed off the hill. As darkness settled over the land, I used the last of the natural light to find my way down to another logging road that followed the creek, hoping it would lead me to the highway or a log to cross over the water, whichever came first.

I pressed the pager button of the walkie-talkie at a rest stop. A delayed annoying ringing shot into the thick spruce forest. I waited for a response from Judy, but only the gurgling of the creek answered. Figuring I was too low in the canyon to get any reception, I put the walkie-talkie back in my pocket. Then I strapped on my headlamp over my hunter-orange hat, spotlighting the narrow two-lane path in the woods, and continued searching for a creek crossing.

A house light at the end of the tunnel of trees told me I finally knew where I was—closing in on the highway and my ticket out of the country where I was starting to feel like I was being held prisoner. I came to a halt, thinking about the possibility that dogs might be guarding the house ahead. Despite the can of bear spray on my hip, my fear of dogs pushed me into making an about-face to scour the streambanks for some log to use to get across the stream.

A ten-minute search took me to a downed tree that spanned the ten-foot-wide creek. I probed the night with my headlamp, assessing my chances of getting across the log without falling and breaking through the ice. It didn't look good. The log's surface, still with its bark on, looked glazed with a thin coating of frosty ice. But getting across the log was only half the problem, as the opposite bank was lined with thick brush. Undoing my waist buckle in case I had to jettison my pack, I stepped up on the spotlit twenty-inch log, crouching like a tiger to make my move across the ice-muffled, bubbling creek. I took a deep breath, eyeing the reflected thin crust of ice I knew wouldn't hold me if I fell, imagining the article in tomorrow's *Missoulian*…

Local man drowns in Bear Creek during Lewis and Clark Reenactment

Even though the likelihood of drowning was slim, I nervously inched my way forward, concentrating hard on stepping on the flattest part of the ice-covered log, slowly making my way to the wall of brush on the other side. Midstream I felt the dizziness from the swift current flowing under a small hole in the ice, but I stayed focused and kept creeping my way across. With relief, I jumped off the log into a thicket of alder, river birch, and redstem ceanothus and slashed my way through the entanglement, making my way out of the canyon bottom and up to the Bear Creek Road.

Blinding headlights bore down on me when I reached the roadcut, as a pickup truck slowed, then came to a stop.

"You out hunting?" a camouflaged hunter asked, spitting tobacco juice out the window.

"I'm hunting for my rig right now," I replied with a frosty breath.

"Saw a little gray pickup 'bout half mile back." More tobacco juice went streaming out the window.

"That's mine!" I announced. "Any luck hunting?"

"Haven't seen a thing."

"Yeah, I haven't seen any game either. Well, see you later," I said knowing that chances were slim I'd ever see him again.

"Yeah…see ya." He spit out the window once more and continued down the road.

After a short walk, gray-painted metal reflections bounced off the rig I was so glad to see. I took off my pack, hopped in my truck, started the engine, and pulled out the map to study tomorrow's route out of Clark Creek.

With the truck warmed up, I did a Y-turn and headed back to *Travelers' Rest II* to prepare to continue on my journey I was so glad had not yet come to an end.

Day 11

November 8, 2002

I picked up where I left off two days ago, parking on Highway 12 and hiking up the Clark Creek logging road following the soothing sound of the creek that stair-stepped its way down the hidden valley, as I made my way beyond my double diamond boot ski run. I could hear machinery from an active timber sale coming from up on the ridge to the southwest. My plan was to hopefully locate the flag line, follow it to the Lewis and Clark Trail, and head west until private property once again turned me around. I'd have to be satisfied with not getting all the way through to Grave Creek.

After a mile-and-a-half search that came up with no evidence of the trail, I stopped and soaked up the beauty of tall golden grass swaying back and forth in the early morning breath of wind, forming waves across the flat twenty-acre meadow valley bottom. Thick puffy gray cumulus clouds hung like huge drapes above the ridges, threatening snow. I could feel the signs of winter in the wind—the cold air, the fact that the birds were flying unusually low.

Not to be denied, I took a mental compass bearing on a fairly noticeable pass high on the ridge to my northwest and headed for it, wading through the tall grass, making my way past a gray-weathered stump remnant of a monster-size pine, then jumping the two-foot-wide stream and crashing through thick brush to the west side of the wide valley floor. Putting it in low gear, I began my steep ascent toward the ridge, crunching my way over fresh logging slash that filled the air with its uniquely sweet-smelling, pungent evergreen scent.

When I arrived at the pass, there still wasn't any sign of the trail. The clouds had become darker, hanging more menacingly over the ridgetops. A quick check of the map showed it to be a good mile and at least two gulches to the private property turn-around spot. Like a man on a mission, I took another quick "bearing" and continued on my quest to find the trail.

Through openings in the tree-lined ridge I could see the head of a dry creekbed a half mile to my northwest. I recalled from the Forest map that the *"Lewis & Clark Trail"* route did not appear to go that far north. The Corps of Discovery's route seemed to cross the gulch about a half mile to the south of the head of the canyon. This would put me in the general location of the trail. I found an opening in the trees, dropped off the ridge, and followed the theoretical line of the historic tread.

The bright yellow wood framed by the black charred burn marks of the old dead snag stood out like a huge piece of gold among the orange puzzle-bark ponderosa pines that dotted the slope. It was a peeled tree, my first positive sign in this area that I had found evidence of the Native path and the Lewis and Clark Trail. I put down my pack and sat down in the grass and brush that guarded the base of the tree, leaning against the snag.

Across the Lolo Creek valley to the south I could see veils of snow sweeping across the sky, dropping their wintry payload over the mountains. I took out my lunch, water, diaries, and the map to enjoy the calm before the storm I knew would soon bear down upon me. As I ate, I reflected back on the Corps of Discovery's journey through this country, reading Patrick Gass's journal entry for September 12, 1805…

"We started early on our journey and had a fine morning. Having travelled 2 miles we reached the mountains which are very steep; but the road over them pretty good, as it is much travelled by the natives, who come across to the Flathead river to gather cherries and berries."

It was an incredible find. So it wasn't just the bison and camas roots the Nez Perce were after when they traveled east on the K'uysey'ne'iskit. It also was the *"cherries and berries"* that lured them to Montana.

A cold wind eddied over the ridge, dropping snow like confetti in a Thanksgiving Day parade, the silver-dollar-size snowflakes soon making the ground wintry white. Quickly I finished my lunch, repacked, and headed up the mountain with new urgency.

I made my way over the ridge and into a gulch, feeling like a land-bound sailboat, leaning hard into the snow-filled, gale-force wind, struggling to go up the steep approach to the ridge above Grave Creek. The wind howled along the top of the divide, as snow-filled, curtains continued to descend upon the land. Plaguing thoughts about getting hypothermia started entering my mind as I neared the private property line. It was the silent killer that stalked a person when they were cold, wet, and tired, as I was now. It *had* almost claimed my life back in 1978, when I had lain down in the snow after a thirty-five-hundred vertical foot tough climb out of the Otter Creek canyon in the wilderness to the east of the firetower. Everything got so peaceful. The cold snow felt like a warm soft cushion to fall asleep upon. So I did go to sleep, dreaming of Judy yelling my name into the thick foggy night from the lookout tower two miles away. Suddenly I woke up, realizing that it *wasn't* a dream, and began my long trudge out of the wilderness, following the voice-in-the-fog calling me home to live another day.

I crested the ridge, peered through squinted eyes into the blinding snow, and discovered a cove of fir trees lower down on the divide. Immediately I took off running like a deer, dropping quickly to the makeshift shelter, and entered the protective hovel of fir boughs. The wintry gale continued to sweep across the ridge as I tore apart my pack to get out my parka, winter gloves, and wind pants.

There was no choice but to wait out the storm, hoping the cloud that clung to the mountain would soon release its grip. Wearing my wintry ensemble, I finally felt like I wasn't going to get hypothermia on this lonely crest of a ridge. The storm continued to howl an eerie tune outside my tree hovel, giving me pause to think what might have happened if the Corps of Discovery had gone through the Bitterroots a little later in the year in 1805. What if the ice on the Missouri River hadn't melted as early as it did, and they had been forced to leave later in the spring from Fort Mandan? What if they had even more trouble than they did going around the Great Falls of the Missouri? What if the Shoshones hadn't given them any horses or let Old Toby serve as their guide? What if the Salish, who the Corps of Discovery met at Ross's Hole in the Bitterroot Valley, hadn't also helped by supplying the Corps with horses? Any one of those things could have delayed their journey through the Bitterroots until late in the fall, when deep snows in the high country might have caused them to retreat to Travelers' Rest to overwinter. But as history proves, near starvation, wet and cold, tired and sick, they did make it to the Weippe Prairie, where they met the Nez Perce who fed them, then regrouped and built dugout canoes to continue their journey to the Pacific. Patrick Gass records for this date in 1805…

"We embarked early. The morning was cloudy, and there was a hard wind from the east. We went about 5 miles and came to a bay 12 or 14 miles wide. We had to coast round it, as the wind raised the waves so high we could go no other way. We halted and dined at a point on the north side of the bay where a small river comes in. We again proceeded on coasting, till we came to a point of land where the bay becomes much narrower; and the water quite salt. The waves here ran so high we were obliged to lie to, and let the tide leave our canoes on dry ground. This point we called Cape Swell; and the bay above, Shallow Bay, as there is no great depth of water."

The wind stopped its angry howl, allowing me a look out at my world. A welcomed break in the clouds was quickly erased by wintry gray. Then another deep blue opening broke through the clouds, which also was wiped away by a puffy cumulus cloud eraser. I was getting a little frustrated as the cold began leaking through my parka. My feet were wet and cold, which once again brought to mind the well-memorized William Clark journal quote… *"I was at one time fearfull my feet would freeze in the thin mockersons which I wore."*

With no more need to be convinced to abandon my search for the historic trail tread, I finally gave up on the weather cooperating and rocketed out of the trees, running as fast as I dared down the mountain toward my truck and the heater I desperately needed right now.

I stopped at the ridge above Clark Creek and watched miniature logging trucks and skidders working a half mile to my south, the sounds of the straining machines drifting up to me. The snow had called a momentary truce, as larger openings of blue dominated the sky. A rainbow arched over Lolo Creek, the collage of red, orange, yellow, green, blue, indigo, and violet melting into the mountains to my south.

Climbing the steep slope above Lolo Creek, heading toward Potato Gulch. (TOP) *Looking east from the ridge above Clark Creek, searching for signs of the historic trail.* (BOTTOM)

Discovering the trail east of Clark Creek by finding an old hidden culturally modified tree.

Flagging that marked recent trail tread in Potato Gulch.

Trail tread in Potato Gulch.

Sheldon Creek.

Arriving at the Sheldon Creek-Smith Creek divide.

One of the many culturally modified trees that led me back on the right path.

An area where the trail disappeared west of Bear Creek. (TOP) *Near the Bear Creek crossing site.* (BOTTOM)

Camp Creek.

Clark Creek meadow where I couldn't find any sign of historic trail tread.

Climbing the mountain above Fort Fizzle, searching for evidence of the historic trails.

High on the ridge to the north of Fort Fizzle.

Looking west from the ridgetop above Lolo Hot Springs, where I lost the trail.

Discovering the trail in the Lolo Hot Springs section.

Entering the Lolo Trail Ranch.

Woodman School as seen from approximate location of the Corps of Discovery's Woodman Camp. (TOP) *Looking northwest from Woodman Camp, with Clark's "Fork on the right" Woodman Creek drainage in the distance.* (BOTTOM)

Following the old wagon road west of Woodman School. (TOP) *Nearing the old Woodman townsite, with "Lewis and Clark Saddle" just to the left of the center of the picture.* (BOTTOM)

The Erickson cabin in the ravine where the Corps of Discovery began their difficult journey "through the Bitterroots". (TOP) Old trap line cubby I found above "Woodman Meadows". (BOTTOM)

At "Woodman Meadows" overlook on the last day of my trek.

At the Lolo Trail Ranch fence line and the end of my Lewis and Clark reenactment journey. (TOP) *Judy discovering some of the historic trail with me on a post journey hike.* (BOTTOM)

Day 12

November 9, 2002

Patrick Gass on November 9, 1805…

"The morning was windy, rainy and disagreeable, and we were obliged to remain at Cape Swell all day and unload our canoes to prevent them from sinking; notwithstanding some of them did sink when the tide came in at noon."

John Crawford…

The morning was cold, windy, and quite *"disagreeable."* I waited until the temperatures moderated, then headed out in the afternoon to finally solve the mystery of the Corps of Discovery's route by Fort Fizzle.

Four miles west from Travelers' Rest, the Corps of Discovery either went up and over the ridges to avoid about a mile of traveling through the brushy Lolo canyon, or they took their chances in the valley bottom. When I biked up the highway on the first day of my trek I didn't have the knowledge I had now, that the Native *"road"* they were following would go over some of the steepest slopes to avoid dealing with the brush. *Did they climb or didn't they?* was the question I wanted to answer as I parked my truck in the Fort Fizzle parking lot.

First, I stopped and reread the interpretive signs, and checked out the log-barrier rifle pit display. Then I bolted like a scared deer across the highway. A short ascent, and I arrived at the actual historical site, where a quick hunt for the rifle pits came up empty. Then I climbed the steeper-than-a-cow's-face mountain to a spine of the ridge and rested, looking out over the valley amidst the rhythm of my wildly beating heart. Isolated tendrils of fog clung to the mountain scene, their milky-white fibrous fingers feeling the tree-covered ridges. Highway 12 looked like a huge black snake stuck in a stationary pose, dividing the fall-cured golden brown meadow on the north side of the valley from the thick green carpet of trees to the south. Burn-scarred dead snags from a human-caused fire in 1988 lay flattened by the wind on their mountainside gravesites. Focusing on the grassy flat below, I noticed the straight lines of the trenches I'd missed on my ground search. I could picture the 1877 scene, with Captain Rawn and troops dug in, waiting in the rifle pits for the non-treaty Nez Perce to come through on their flight east heading toward Canada. Buildings from a private residence to the south stood like miniature models from an electric train set near the base of the ridge where the Nez Perce had begun their steep ascent from Lolo Creek to avoid the troops.

I continued my climb up the spine, skirting around downed logs, and keeping a close eye out for any scalloped-edged trees or signs of old trail tread. The subtle depressions that followed the ridge I guessed could have been from the one-time passage on the Nez Perce Trail. But I wasn't convinced yet that this wasn't also their "Trail to the Buffalo Country" route, so I climbed higher.

Gaining most of the elevation to the highest point on the ridge, the view opened to a grand vista. Framed by the wide notch of the Lolo valley, mountains to the east stood posed, freshly frosted with snow. Lolo Peak* stood impressive to the southwest, its steep rocky gray flanks showing through the early signs of winter. An unnamed gulch to the east lay hidden, just over the crest of the ridge. I was about a thousand vertical feet above the valley floor, which I was now convinced was much too high for millenniums of Native travelers and the Corps of Discovery explorers to have climbed just to avoid a mile of a brushy canyon bottom. For the Nez Perce fleeing Captain Howard, though, it was their only way to get around the troops hiding in the flats below.

Taking a logging road through the head of *No Name Gulch*, I came to an abrupt drop into Sawmill Gulch. I could hardly imagine the Nez Perce going down this slope—the old, the women and children, and the

* There are two summits that are referred to as "Lolo Peak". The south summit is the official Lolo Peak at 9,096 feet. The "unofficial" north summit reaches 8,694 feet. I am referring to the north peak here and on p.156.

wounded. But they *did* go down that extremely steep slope on July 28, 1877, skirting around the volunteer and regular army troops, and making it to Sleeman Gulch and through the Bitterroot Valley, heading for the Big Hole.

I took off heading south, hiking along a fairly gentle ridge, returning to the valley floor. Soon I came to a halt at the top of another double-diamond boot-ski run. I gave some thought to contouring down into *No Name Gulch* to access the ridge I had hiked coming up the mountain. But I also thought, *Am I going to chicken out shooting down an easier looking slope than what the Nez Perce went down?*

I stood at the top of the straight shot into the canyon like a skier who was looking down a run he'd never dream of attempting in his right mind. Patches of snow clung to the frozen mountainside, looking like perfect launching pads for taking a flight toward the highway. Scattered ice-glazed rocks could also send me cart-wheeling down the mountain. The late afternoon cloud-filtered sunlight was quickly being replaced by early evening dusty gray, pushing my decision to take the fast route, as I jumped over the edge, initiating my boot-ski run down the steep, slippery slope.

With the decision to gain more control than I had on the Clark Creek boot-ski run, I did a half-run, half-slide routine across the frozen slope, checking my speed as I whizzed past the slippery rocks and snow pillows. Working my way down the mountain, I zigzagged toward the valley floor.

I skidded to a stop above a snow-filled scree slope. A hundred feet and I'd be down and wading through the grassy flat canyon bottom. One misstep, and I could be frantically waving down traffic on the highway to rescue me after a slip and nasty fall. There didn't seem to be a choice other than going through the scree that wrapped the base of the mountain like a moat around a castle.

I stepped down on a snow-covered flat rock, starting a miniature rockslide cascading down the mountainside. Then another slide avalanched down with another tenuous step. Forgetting style points, I got down on all fours and crab-walked the rest of my way to the toe of the slope.

Back at the truck I looked up at the silhouette of the high ridge across the valley, where I could *see* the Nez Perce heading east in peace.

November 10-15, 2002

A change of plans pushed my search for the Lolo Hot Springs trail section back a week, after I returned from work on the Selway.

Day 13

November 16, 2002

Five inches of snow had fallen during the morning with no sign of letting up, and temperatures were dropping like a rock. I knew I had to hike the Lolo Hot Springs section before winter shut me down for good. With my daypack stuffed with survival gear, I headed out the door dressed for the Arctic. Judy and I exchanged waves as I drove out of the driveway into the blinding snowstorm.

I was on my way to solve another trail mystery. The first time through the confusing country of every-which-way ridges and draws and look-alike hills by the hot springs, I had gotten lost. But on my last visit with trail expert, Kevin Foss, he insisted the trail *did* exist because he had hiked it.

I pulled off the plowed highway, cutting tracks in the snow on the side of the road. Keeping the engine running and the defroster on high, I brought out the map. The steady *flap flap flap* of the windshield wipers cleared my view to the west from the quarter-size snowflakes. I was a couple hundred yards east of the Spring Gulch Road, where I had begun my earlier search for the phantom trail. The map seemed to show the trail cutting across Spring Gulch a couple hundred yards up from the mouth of the canyon. But Kevin's description put it much closer to the highway. The first time through here, I had figured the tree-covered mountainslope was much too steep for a trail. But now, as I sat staring at the mountain through the snowflakes peacefully floating to the ground, I realized maybe it *wasn't* too steep after all. I had huffed and puffed my way up the steepest of Native trail braids on my trek. This slope surely wouldn't have stopped the Native Americans from putting the path here.

I put down the map on the dash and picked up the journals, referring back to William Clark's description of September 13, 1805, the day they headed west from *8 PM Camp*...

"a cloudy morning Capt Lewis and one of our guides lost their horses, Capt Lewis & 4 men detained to hunt the horses, I proceeded on with the partey up the Creek at 2 miles passed Several Springs which I observed the Deer Elk &c. had made roads to, and below one of the Indians had made a whole to bathe, I tasted this water and found it hot & not bad tasted."

I drove up the highway a hundred yards and pulled into a wide spot at the bottom of the Spring Gulch Road. I cut the ignition and locked the door, initiating my search for the Lewis and Clark Trail. A hundred feet up the road I noticed a very small piece of the familiar brown-and-orange striped flagging dangling from a bush on the left side of the logging road, which I must have missed on my first trail search. "All...right!" I yelled out, throwing my arms up in a victory celebration for finding the clue I had been looking for. But where *was* the trail? Below the tiny ribbon was a thick wall of brush, with no obvious openings for a trail. Unfazed, I dropped off the roadcut, crashed through the brush and climbed out of the thicket on the other side. Like a mirage, the missing trail appeared in front of me. The mystery of where the hot springs trail started had finally been solved.

Excited, I slipped my way up the well-defined path, feeling the connection to Lewis and Clark come alive again. At an opening in the trees, I looked down at the black ribbon of asphalt cutting through the snow-draped spruces and firs. The snowstorm had made its way east, the wintry white veil caressing the ridges farther down the valley. I took a picture, grabbed a snack, and proceeded west into unexplored-by-me country.

Short of the ridgetop the trail disappointingly gave out, with no more flagging showing. I waded through the snow, searching for some clue that would lead me back to the path, arriving a hundred yards later at an undeveloped road at the crest of the ridge, which brought out another check of the map. The road I was on didn't show up, but a large section of private hot springs land stood like a huge locked gate blocking passage on the Lewis and Clark Trail for about the next mile. From what I could tell, the Fish Creek Road appeared to mark part of the western boundary of the property. I needed to find the north private property line and follow it west to the road. From there I could jog around to the south and pick up the trail again. I put away the map and continued punching through five inches of fluffy powder among snow-splashed tree trunks of majestic ponderosa pines just to the west of the road. Suddenly a snow-muffled engine sound broke the deep silence of the winter-hushed land. I held up, watching an SUV appear through the trees, slowly coming in my direction. The rig stopped a couple hundred feet to the south of me and the engine died as I saw someone roll down the passenger-side window. **"You are on private property! You must leave immediately!"** a woman yelled with a commanding voice across the ridgetop.

"Sorry!" I shouted back through the pine trees that stood like huge statues over the flat ridge. "I didn't know exactly where the private property line was!" I waited patiently for details about how to get back on Forest Service land, but only an uneasy silence filled the crisp, cold air. I cupped my hands around my mouth and yelled louder, "Where ***is*** the private property line?" Another long, tense silence filled the air. After finally figuring out I wasn't going to get an answer, I made fast tracks through the tree giants heading north, away from the private property. Apparently what I did worked, as I heard the engine start up and saw the SUV slip through the snowy landscape in the direction of Spring Gulch. Paralleling the old logging road for another hundred yards and not finding any fence lines or signs to prove I was on private property, I started hiking cross-country to the west. Patrick Gass related in his journal entry of September 13, 1805…

"There are so many paths leading to and from this spring, that our guide took a wrong one for a mile or two, and we had bad travelling across till we got into the road again."

Like a bad dream, I ended up not being able to locate the north property boundary and went on another wild goose chase through the confusing, gently rolling country that all looked the same. After weaving a wavy line of boot tracks between the snow-covered fir and pine trees for a good mile, I surprisingly topped out on the same ridge overlooking Granite Creek where I had been on my first time through this country. I gazed out over the landscape of look-alike ridges, hills, and valleys freshly blanketed with seven inches of snow. Except for the snow it probably was the same scene the Corps of Discovery saw when they came through nearly two hundred years ago. Curtains of snow-filled fog hung in the distance, connecting earth with the gray opaque sky.

I slid on my butt down a snow chute and made my way to the bridge that had escorted me out of this country on my previous search for the trail through here. The chattering of a water ouzel quickly turned to its patented flute-like notes as a *whooooosh* came down from a heavy snow-laden tree branch, releasing its load to the soft white blanket on the ground. This could have been the same spot where the Corps of Discovery ended up after taking one of the *"many paths"* from the hot springs area. Traveling up Granite Creek from the pools would have been an easy mistake. I had been funneled into this spot twice now in less than a month. Maybe the same thing happened to them. Could it be possible that by getting lost I replicated their 1805 trip west more than I thought? If only I could talk to the ghosts of the past who made their way through here on September 13, 1805.

I wadded up a snowball and tossed it off the bridge, listening to a *ker…plunk* as a growing circle of ripples raced for the streambanks. Readjusting my daypack, I headed out, hiking south on the road, following a set of parallel ruts in the snow as darkening gray shadows cast over the land.

Just like the Corps of Discovery on September 13, 1805, I hiked at least *"for a mile or two,"* before I rejoined *"the road again"* at the trailhead a couple hundred yards to the north of Highway 12. At this same spot where I'd picked up the trail heading west back in October, I had a decision to make. Either I could make a quick exit to the highway and walk back to my truck at Spring Gulch, or I could try to locate the *phantom* trail that headed east. The quickly drawing curtain of darkness gave me the answer I needed, so I made tracks in the snow for Highway 12, following the softly lit glow of the Lolo Hot Springs Resort lights reflecting off low-hanging clouds.

As I walked along the north side of the highway, the sound of hundreds of geese honking overhead held me spellbound, bringing me to an abrupt halt. I arched my neck and stared into the night at the ghostly silhouettes of snow geese, their frantically beating wingtips touching the bottoms of the thick ceiling of clouds. The sky pulsated with fluctuating waves of geese circling above the resort's lights, which seemed to be attracting them like a giant beacon. After a couple of minutes of being hypnotized by the powerful migrational force, I took off running toward the source of the lights to share this mesmerizing sight with my "little brother".

I burst into the hot springs pool door. "Hey, Carl!" I snagged his attention away from the computer.

"Well, hi John!" He got up from his chair and walked over to the counter to shake my hand.

"You should see what's going on outside right now!" I exclaimed in a raspy, out-of-breath voice.

"What?" he answered with a confused look on his face.

"There are geese everywhere!"

A woman and young girl walked in. "Be back with you in a minute, John," Carl said politely, turning on his professional pool-manager manner.

"You bet, Carl," I replied, racing back outside. Hundreds of cloud-muted honks were going off, the geese continuing to circle over the lights that cast an eerie orange glow into the night. Waves of white-wing reflections of snow geese mixed with the gray of Canada geese, their erratic flight patterns weaving into ever-changing V's etching across the dull orange-painted sky. After a quick glance back to the pool, noticing the customers had gone, I made my break for the door.

I threw open the glass entry, catching the presence of *another* customer on my periphery coming from the shower area as I headed to the counter. Frantic to find my "little brother", I discovered Carl was nowhere in sight. *Where did he go?* I asked myself. The customer was coming closer, shadowing me. "Say, I'm looking for the guy who runs the pool?" I asked as I turned around and embarrassingly discovered Carl was "the shadow."

"I was wondering what the heck was going on," Carl simply stated in the epitome of Marine *remain-calm* attitude he had from eight years in the Corps.

"Carl, you've got to go outside and see those geese!" I exclaimed in *the-farthest-thing-from-a-calm* voice.

My "little brother" joined me as we stared into the sky, gazing up at the many flocks of honking geese honing in on the resort's lights. Neither one of us talked as we stayed entranced by the undulating waves of wings, our spirits flying high with them. It was a present to share with Carl, a gift of a memory that would last forever.

Another customer drove in, so I said goodbye and headed east, hiking along the highway to my truck at the mouth of Spring Gulch. Without a headlamp I continued my communion with nature, listening to the honking of the geese, seeing every wingbeat and feeling every pulse that seemed to beat from the very heart of nature.

JANUARY 29, 2003

The long wait for the January thaw to melt the lower elevation snow, and my not wanting my trip to come to an end, caused the two-and-a-half-month delay in completing the *Woodman Meadows* final leg of my journey. My procrastination also led me back to where my expedition began in October, as I turned off of Highway 93 onto Mormon Creek Road. It was a cool day and the sky was a huge bowl of high wispy cirrus clouds. Snow-covered Lolo Peak stood majestic, peeking above the shoulder of Carlton Ridge. I saw a *Lewis and Clark Real Estate* "For Sale" sign. Then the sign I was looking for appeared. I had returned to Travelers' Rest State Park three months after I had started my journey. The Corps of Discovery, on this date in 1806, was still in Oregon waiting out the winter at Fort Clatsop. I read the information sign...

Attention Visitors
Please check in with
today's docent at the
garage. Thank you

Letting off the brakes, I drove through the wagon-wheel-framed entrance and down the hundred-yard driveway to the park. I pulled into a circular drive by the garage turned makeshift visitor center, got out and read the magic-marker board attached to the garage siding.

Welcome to Travelers'
Rest State Park
Refreshments in the house.
Parking in the hayfield behind you.
No smoking please

I got back in my truck, moved it to the muddy flat, parking between an SUV and a small sedan. There were no signs of life. Temptation to take them up on their invitation to go into the warm house was quickly countered by my ethics of being the Lewis and Clark explorer type that I was. Give me the cold, and add a blizzard. Throw in some tough stream crossings or a hard-to-find, steep, brushy, downfall-and-root-wad-laced trail. A warm, heated house! Heck, I'd take being out in this cold any day to feel what the 1800s explorers felt! The *"Refreshments in the house"* line on the sign, though, made me question my hard-line reenactment ethics. But the Corps of Discovery didn't have *refreshments-to-go* when they came through in 1805 and 1806. There was no Wagon Wheel Pizza, Harvest Foods grocery store, or Lolo Super Stop. The tough and hardy Lewis and Clark party had only what little game they could find and the dry provisions they brought along.

Even though the sign did welcome me to the house, I stayed with my ethics, walking to the garage and letting myself into the self-service visitor center. There was an unplugged space heater on the concrete slab. Some handouts and a visitor register were on a small table near the door. A map of the Lewis and Clark journey hung on the wall. I documented my visit, grabbed a couple of handouts, and made my way back outside into the *warmer* air.

With nobody from the house checking on their one and only visitor, I was all alone. But being by myself was what I wanted to *feel* at the spot where the Corps of Discovery rested on their westward and eastward journeys across the continent. A chainlink fence wrapped the small yard of the white shiplapped house. Large non-native elms stood guard just inside the fence. A modern two-story house stood off to the southeast, contrasted by an old large brown-stained barn to the southwest. Houses piggybacked up the hills. Trailers dotted the landscape to the west. A dog barked. Jet contrails drew huge tic-tac-toe lines across the sky. I heard the *tap tap tap* of a hammer, backdropped by the constant *whooshing* of nonstop traffic from Highway 93. A car engine started up. I wandered to the back of the house, leaving the 21st century behind.

I stood on a bench overlooking the knapweed-and-grass-covered flat where the Corps of Discovery had camped. A cathedral of cottonwoods arched over Lolo Creek as it wound its way through the valley a hundred yards to my north. Two hundred years ago the stream channel was different, an oxbow tree-lined dry creekbed showing where the water once flowed. Lewis and Clark's campsite was just south of the perfect horseshoe-shaped bend in the old streambed. I could imagine them standing by the central cooking fire, with Old Toby telling stories, and comparing trail notes through the many interpreters of how they would get through the Bitterroots in mid-September of 1805. Then I wound the clock ahead to late June and early July of 1806, *listening* to the Corps trying to work out the next-to-impossible logistics of splitting up and meeting in about a month at the confluence of the Missouri and Yellowstone Rivers.

Going east from Travelers' Rest was just as much a challenge for the Corps of Discovery as it had been heading west. Backtracking the same way they came through Montana in 1805 would have been hard enough. But in 1806 they were dividing their already small party to explore even more of the uncharted west. How did they even think there was a chance of meeting in the middle of nowhere after a longer-than-a-month journey through this wilderness? Lewis's route, which would include an exploration of the Marias River, went through mostly unfamiliar country after heading north from Travelers' Rest. Clark's route was going through unfamiliar country after branching off their old route, heading for the Yellowstone River. But as history records, both groups reached the confluence of the two rivers within a week of each other. There Lewis found a note from Clark attached to a pole on August 7th, explaining that he had gone ahead because there wasn't much game and the mosquitoes were bad. On Clark's heels, Lewis met up with his friend five days later, nearly six weeks after they left Travelers' Rest, joining forces on August 12, 1806, near where the Little Missouri River flows into the Missouri River in present day North Dakota.

I took another look around. The trees without their dancing leaves stood naked to the sky, the mountains showing through their bare arms. I could see the ridge coming down across the valley, forming the barrier that Lewis and company went around on their short northward jog before heading east toward the Rocky Mountain front on July 3, 1806. To the west the steep walls of the Lolo Creek canyon shouldered against the cirrus-clouded pale blue sky.

Sad to have another chapter come to an end, I wandered back to the front of the house and my pickup parked in the muddy flat. I opened the door, got in and cranked down the window. A collage of modern-day sounds floated through the air—the tree-muffled traffic, the staccato beats of hammering from a nearby construction site, and an orange-faded windsock hanging from an electric pole flapping in the wind. Then I closed my eyes and *heard* the echoes of the past canceling out the sounds of the present. I turned the key in the ignition and pulled out of the parking lot, merging back into the 21st century.

January 31, 2003

A cold hard rain continued to delay my final day on the trail, rerouting my trek to Fort Missoula and a visit with Milo McLeod, the Lolo National Forest Archaeologist.

Excitement built as I wandered through a maze of office cubicles, making my way to the man who possibly knew more than anyone about the history of the Lolo Trail. The Lolo Trail is an encompassing term which includes the "K'uysey'ne'iskit" or the "Trail to the Buffalo Country", the "Naptnišá" or the "Trail to the Nez Perce", the Nez Perce (Nee-Me-Poo or Nimiipuu) National Historic Trail and Lewis and Clark National Historic Trail, the Bird-Truax Wagon Road, and the Lolo Motorway. A slide show that Milo gave about the trail the night before prompted more questions and the reason for my follow-up visit.

"Milo…John Crawford." Our hands locked in a firm handshake. "Glad I caught you in."

"Have a seat." He pointed to a chair next to his desk.

I brought out a notebook, sitting down across from him. "I sure did enjoy your slide show last night."

"Thanks!"

"Say, I've got some questions about the trail that I was hoping you might be able to answer. Mind if I borrow a pen?"

"Sure thing." He handed me a blue Bic.

"Haven't seen rain like this the middle of winter in years," I commented. "Makes me feel like I'm at Fort Clatsop."

"Yeah, it sure is wet."

Small talk quickly turned to trail talk, Milo picking up where he left off at the previous evening's slide talk at the Missoula Public Library, telling me about his background on the Lolo Trail, and the mountainmen, explorers, miners, and railroad surveyors who used the trail since Lewis and Clark. He explained more about the attempts to make a wagon road all the way through from Lewiston to Lolo in the mid-1860s. He talked about the "Flight of the Nez Perce" in 1877 to escape Captain Howard and how they followed the Bird-Truax Wagon Road, which diverted in some areas from the route of the "K'uysey'ne'iskit" and the "Naptnišá"—the history of the Lolo Trail coming alive on the last of the gray January days in his second-story office in the old army fort west of Missoula.

The peeled tree pictures I brought with me triggered more excitement about the Lolo Trail, spawning more conversation, feeding our common interest, keeping the discussion going past normal Forest Service quitting time, past the time when most personnel are rushing out the door and racing home for the weekend. But Milo stayed glued to his seat, as I was glued to mine...our common interest continuing to build with our mutual excitement of talking about a trail that was a part of both of us. I learned that my north-side-of-the-valley, toe-of-the-slope trail placement theory to avoid the brush was correct. The braided-trails-paralleling-the-main-trail-trench theory was correct. The Native American hatchet- or knife-carved, scalloped-edged peeled trees, I found out, were known as "culturally modified trees" by archeologists. A mutual love for a trail kept us talking and trading notes on a history that seemed as alive today as it had been nearly two hundred years ago. I saw it in his eyes and heard it in his voice...the Lolo Trail had transformed Milo as much as it had me. As I left his office I realized the spirit of the trail was alive and growing in both of our souls.

I drove away from the Fort, weaving around the old red-tile roofed buildings, splashing through curb-dammed rainwater puddles and thinking about the future of my Lewis and Clark trek that was hewn down to only one more day. The end of my journey was now on hold, waiting for the rainstorm to move east so I could finish the *Woodman Meadows* section. I would hike this last section slowly, taking in the trail like a fine wine, absorbing every last inch of the Lewis and Clark Trail I had been following in my mind for years. If I had my way, I would make the final tread last *forever*.

Day 14

February 2, 2003

Twinkling little jewels of starlight just before dawn told me the weather had finally cleared enough to make my move to complete the final leg of my journey. But along with other Americans, today I had a heavy heart thinking about the seven astronauts who died the day before in the *Columbia* Space Shuttle tragedy. So things went a little slow this morning. I drove down to Lolo at a snail's pace, picked up a newspaper and a half-gallon of milk at Harvest Foods, then drove back home even more slowly, a few other early risers flying by me like I was practically standing still.

Then it was coffee and muffins with Judy, my support crew of one, getting filled in on my last day's trekking plans. After receiving permission to hike on ranch land by the school, I would hike from the Corps of Discovery's *Woodman Camp* and follow their toe-of-the-slope route through the valley. At the west end of *Woodman Meadows* I would head into the mountains, hopefully connecting with the fence line that had turned me around on Day 10 of my journey, east of Camp Creek. William Clark described leaving the meadows on September 12, 1805…

"at 2 miles assended a high hill & proceeded through a hilley and thickly timbered Countrey…"

I had spent the last three months studying the map and staring at the notch in the ridge where the trail went through. The route was memorized, locked in my psyche. It was a piece-of-cake hike. I *wouldn't* need a map.

The timetable had been set. Before noon I would check with the Lolo Trail Ranch foreman about hiking on the land. After noon I would set off from Woodman School, timing my hike so I would be at the meadow overlook in the best sunlight for taking pictures. Judy would keep tabs on my progress with our walkie-talkie communication, and stand by for word that I was ready to be shuttled back to my truck.

The first hint that maybe things wouldn't go quite according to plan was the *BEWARE OF DOGS* sign I saw as I slowly made my way up the driveway of the Lolo Trail Ranch. I slowed to a crawl, my truck barely moving as I frantically searched for a place to turn around to make my escape. It was too late. The dog *welcoming committee* was fast approaching, barking menacingly to protect their turf. I raced through the options. I could back up a quarter mile to the highway or I could continue courting disaster with the dogs. Flipping a coin in my mind, I chose plan B, and continued making my way up the half-mile-long driveway, the dogs barking out the message loud and clear…*YOU ARE MAKING A HUGE MISTAKE!*

I stopped in front of the ranch foreman's residence and remained in my truck, the engine idling, and the dogs still loudly barking. There was no sign of anybody around. Then I saw movement out of the corner of my eye, as a young woman approached from the ranch-style log house. I rolled down the window, too afraid to chance a dog mauling by getting out. The incessant barking slowed to an occasional yap.

"Hi! My name's John Crawford and I'm your neighbor from down the valley a ways. I was wondering if Jim Haydon is around because I'd like to get his permission to hike on the ranch land," I announced to the woman who stood outside the truck door. I turned the key, the engine coughing out a complaint, then dying.

"He's not here right now," she replied, shushing one of the dogs that didn't get the hint I wasn't a threat. "Can I help you? I'm Jim's wife, Shari." We shook hands.

"Yeah. I'm following the Lewis and Clark Trail through the Lolo valley and I just have the ranch section left to hike to finish it. I'm planning on writing a book about my experiences."

Shari's eyes lit with interest. "Oh, that's really neat!"

"My partner, Judy, and I have lived in the valley for over twenty years. She teaches over at Woodman School. I wrote this book for the school's Centennial celebration back in 1992." I repeated the words I had memorized from my morning dress rehearsal, handing her a copy of ***The Woodman Echo*** with my name on it to verify my claim. She paged through it. "There's some pictures of Judy and her class in it, and some of the ranch."

"The ranch?"

"Yeah. I've got that section marked," I said as she opened the book to the 1938 photo of the Van Ostrand family posed in front of their old log cabin bunkhouse. "Roy Van Ostrand, who owns Thistle Dew Antiques down the road, used to live here." Shari studied the picture. "And you know, I bet the cabin over there is the same one that's in the book," I explained, pointing to an old small log cabin a couple hundred feet to the west.

"Think so?"

"Most likely."

"The Ozmuns would sure love a copy of this book!" she commented, handing it back to me.

I recognized the ranch owner's name. "I'll make sure to give them one when we print another edition."

"They'd sure like that," she paused, shushing one of the dogs that started to bark again. "Go ahead. You're welcome to hike on the land!" she said with a definite hint of excitement in her voice. "Just watch out for the cattle. They might be a little ornery this time of year."

"I'll definitely keep an eye out for them!" I answered, giddy as a little kid at Christmas time. "And I'll get you a copy of the Lewis and Clark book if I can ever get it published."

"Thanks a lot!"

"You bet!"

"Oh…and just one more thing!" she announced before I rolled the window all the way up. "You'll also run into dogs at the other ranch houses. I'll call and let folks know you'll be coming through."

"Are they chained?" I asked with an undercurrent of fear in my wavering voice, scared stiff at the thought about being chased by mad dogs *without* the protection of two tons of steel.

"Oh they're fenced. You won't have to worry about a thing!"

Famous last words! I thought to myself. "Thanks a lot for letting me hike on the land. I'll try to locate Lewis and Clark's *Woodman Camp* and follow the trail to the west fence line."

"Well, have a good hike!"

"Thanks." I rolled up the window, started the truck and drove over to the little log cabin.

I stared at the old gray walls. Then I studied the picture in ***The Woodman Echo***. They had the same roof pitches and appeared to be the same size. Five people sat and three stood in front of the building, most of the Van Ostrand family, Roy's niece, and one visitor. Small-diameter logs were stacked just above the window. A quick look at the book and I could tell they were a perfect match, the at-least-sixty-five-year-old cabin verified in a minute of well-spent time.

I drove down the long driveway amid the grandeur of the huge ponderosa pine trees overshadowing the parklike land around the ranch buildings, and the sweeping vistas of the Lolo valley with the little white schoolhouse sitting peacefully on the grassy bench across the canyon. I merged with the highway, returning to *Travellers Rest II* to prepare for my last day of following the explorers who had passed through here nearly two hundred years ago. By nightfall my journey would be over.

"So, let's see if I have this right," Judy began as President Bush *watched us* with a permanent *I-mean-business* pose from a poster on the wall above the chalkboard. "You want me to meet you on the highway at the west end of *Woodman Meadows*?" she asked, handing out papers onto the empty desks that sat underneath large suspended snowflake art projects hanging from a wire stretched across the classroom.

"Yeah."

"Explain again what you mean by *Woodman Meadows*."

"The cattle pasture west of the old Woodman townsite," I responded, peering out the window, looking for any winter hawk residents circling above the steep foothills in back of the school. "On second thought," I paused, "just go with our original plan and keep the walkie-talkie turned on so I can let you know when I want to be picked up."

"Sounds good." More papers got handed out to the invisible Sunday afternoon class. "Just be careful out there! You *do* have a map?"

"Don't need one!" I said confidently. "Believe me, I know where I'm going. You don't need to worry!" Our eyes met as she stopped ferrying papers. "I *won't* get lost!"

A send-off wave to Judy at the front schoolhouse double doors and I was off, making my way down the concrete steps, initiating the final chapter in my Lewis and Clark journey. My first stop was the Corps' *Woodman Camp*. Clark noted on September 11, 1805… *"Encamped at Some old Indian Lodges, nothing killed this evening hills on the right high & ruged, the mountains on the left high & Covered with Snow."*

I headed to where I thought Clark's journal entry was leading me — down the school drive, across the highway, through a gate in the ranch fence, over an irrigation ditch, and to a bend in the creek.

Woodman School stood across the valley, the 1902 steep-pitched-roof schoolhouse standing like a small white church at the base of the *"hills on the right high & ruged."* The ranch buildings were nestled in the majestic pines on the south side of the valley, at the base of the *"mountains on the left high & Covered with Snow."* Lolo Creek rushed by my feet. A hawk soared above the school. Semi trucks, pickups and sedans roared by on the highway a couple hundred feet away. It was a mixing of cultures, a blending of the times. I blocked out the highway traffic and concentrated on the past, feeling the presence of the Corps of Discovery who had camped here or somewhere very close nearly two hundred years ago. It was a magical, special moment knowing that I was possibly standing where they stood, *seeing* close to what they saw, *hearing* some of what they heard, perhaps *feeling* a little what they felt. I looked across the valley again and focused on the school that was 110 years old and counting. It stood as a connection to the past: the children going to Woodman School absorbing the valley's rich, colorful past while gaining the knowledge that would help them grow into the future.

I dug out the journal from my pack, feeling the history come alive again from the trail-worn pages. Clark described on the morning of September 12, 1805…

"a white frost Set out at 7 oClock & proceeded on up the Creek, passed a Fork on the right on which I saw near an old Indian encampment a Swet house Covered wthh earth."

John Crawford on February 2, 2003…Fresh snow in the hills. Set out at 2:30 p.m. and proceeded to hike across the ranch field toward the *"Fork on the right."*

Heading for the toe of the slope on the north side of the valley, I recrossed the highway and kept my eyes open for any ornery cattle the ranch foreman's wife had warned me about. Quick surveys proved the golden grassy pastures were clear of any cattle as far as I could see to the west. A couple of redtail hawks danced in the wind above the ridge, their large wings casting dark silhouettes against the blue and cloud-mottled sky. The wind whispered a peaceful tune through the pines.

I stopped at the old wagon road, which followed the old Native *"road"* and the Lewis and Clark Trail at the toe of the slope of the steep dry hills. The notch in the ridge to the west, which I dubbed *Lewis and Clark Saddle*, was perched about four hundred vertical feet above the end of the valley floor. It looked like an easy two-hour hike away. A quick, futile check for any evidence of the original 1892 log cabin school that had burned at the turn of the century, and I headed west on the final leg of my trek.

It was a culmination of a life-long dream to be hiking up one of the most beautiful valleys in Montana, following the explorers who epitomized *out west* exploration. Lolo Peak, at over nine thousand feet, capped with deep winter snows, stood majestically above the valley. If I had been an early-day settler, this is the area where I would have staked my claim just as Tony Zens had done in the 1930s. When he arrived in the Lolo Creek valley he looked around and claimed, *"This is heaven on earth"*. A mile southeast of the school he had lived in an old log cabin, and had become a trapper. He never *really* left the valley, as his old traps still dangle from his gravesite at the base of the mountain where his trapline began.

I approached my first barrier to any more westward travel. *Tick tick tick*, the temporary electric fence was "hot". A stretched wire gate was my only access, so I tried to release the pressure on the wire lassoed around a wooden stave. No luck…it wouldn't budge. I followed the temporary fence line to the north foothills to find another gate opening, but came up with no other way through. I returned to the gate and saw a wooden pallet leaning up against the fence that I felt could be used as a ladder. *Tick tick tick.* I jabbed my rubber-soled winter boot into a knee-high slot in the pallet. *Tick tick tick.* Springing like a scared cat I went flying over the gate, landing on the other side in a two-point acrobatic stance. It wasn't pretty, but effective. Then I continued on, hiking west along the old wagon road ruts…following the ghosts of the past.

Dry gulches, dotted with pines and junipers, cut into the steep slope to my right. I checked the large ponderosa pines to see if any were culturally modified trees, but came up empty. Fenced hay storage was at the mouth of one of the gulches and a covered galvanized feeder bunk sat at the mouth of another. Clouds broke apart and re-formed, the countryside bathed in short bursts of golden sunlight. Woodman Hill arched its evergreen back across the valley to the southwest.

"John, do you have a copy?" Judy's voice shot out from my pocket. I grabbed the little black leather-cased walkie-talkie and held it above my head for better reception. "John! Do you read me, over?"

I pushed the transmitter button. "Yeah Judy, I read you."

"I'm leaving now. How's it going out there?"

"Had a little problem getting over a fence, but otherwise everything's going great!"

"How far are you?"

"About a mile from the school, just below the old Woodman gravesite."

"Oh yeah. I can see you over there! I'll keep the radio on at the house, waiting for your call."

"Sounds great." I waved at the school, at what I thought was a tiny figure of Judy.

"If I don't get a call within a few hours, I'll drive up the highway looking for you."

"Yeah, good idea."

"You be careful out there!"

"Don't you worry about a thing. I'll be fine. See you later, teacher lady!"

"See you later, mister explorer."

I put the small black box back in my pocket and looked up at the rail-fenced gravesite. Dan and Elizabeth Woodman, the Lachman twins, and Sarah Wilkinson—some of the early Woodman residents who were buried there—lay in peace on the hillside above me like century-old guardians of the valley.

Approaching the white, single-story hip-roofed ranch house that stood at the old Woodman townsite, I went on full scale alert for the protector of the residence who lay curled up sleeping on the front fenced-in lawn. I reached into my pocket, feeling the trigger on the can of OC-10 that would be my last defense in case of a dog charge. There was a ghost town feel in the air, the increasing afternoon wind singing an eerie tune through the naked arms of the old stately cottonwood trees. As stealthily as possible, I made my way west along the old wagon road ruts a hundred feet away from the chainlink fence that stood as the only protection between me and the Rottweiler that suddenly jumped up, growling viciously! The huge black-and-brown-mottled attack dog began his charge, racing to the short fence it could easily breach in one good leap. I picked up my pace, trying to put as much distance between us as possible, hoping he would stop the barking that sounded like he wanted to eat me for lunch. He kept up the verbal attack; my heart keeping perfect beat with the barks...***Boom Boom Boom Boom Boom Boom!*** My stride became a jog, as I constantly looked back, thanking God that the chainlink fence psychological barrier was working.

After a couple hundred yards of buffer and crossing Clark's *"Fork on the right"* Woodman Creek, I finally caught my breath. The dog's bark was becoming less frequent, my finger releasing from the spray can trigger as my heart stopped feeling like it was about to pound out of my chest. One dog down, another house of dogs only a quarter mile away. I had about ten minutes to relax.

An old weathered stump above the wagon road caught my eye. There was a familiar-looking carved-out section at its base. I hurried over to it, verifying in an instant my guess that it was a culturally modified tree remnant of the *"Indian encampment"* William Clark had referred to in his journal. Another old peeled gray-weathered tree stump nearby confirmed the Native village and the trail that led into the mountains to the west. I catalogued the tree locations in my mind and continued along the old wagon road.

My trek through the valley was almost over. Another quarter mile and I would enter the mountains where Clark described on September 12, 1805, they *"assended a high hill."* I had studied the route every trip back and forth on the highway going to work at the ranger station in Idaho. It looked like a piece-of-cake hike up a small ravine in back of the next ranch house, leading to *Lewis and Clark Saddle*. From the saddle, the map I had memorized showed one more gulch to the west before I would get to the barbwire fence that halted my advance eastward on November 7. It was an easy hike if I could get by the two dogs that were already barking out very loud and clear...*TURN AROUND BEFORE IT'S TOO LATE!* Fear gripped me as I frantically dug in my pack and got out the pepper spray to add to my OC-10 anti-dog weaponry. My fingers played with the plastic triggers of the two pressurized metal cans in my pockets while I did a detour around the barking dog duo, winding my way through some stately ponderosa pine trees to the south of the brown-and-white modular house. They barked in unison, intensifying their *TURN AROUND* message. I fumbled with another wire loop gate latch, which luckily had enough slack and opened. A car came up the long dirt driveway from the highway. I nervously waved at the young woman in the little blue sedan who returned the greeting, apparently forewarned by Shari that I wasn't an intruder. The consequences of her not knowing who I was and what I was up to might have had me facing a shotgun problem in addition to the dog problem. Still barking, growling, and snarling, the dogs gave me the two best *reasons* to keep up my detour a hundred yards to the south, passing the mouth of the gulch where the spirits of Lewis and Clark yelled, *Take a right, Crawford!* But turning right would have meant a turn for the worst, the route going right by the two madly barking dogs. So I did an end run around the canines, circling to the west and climbing the ridge above the gulch.

It worked. The barking turned to an occasional yap, then to silence as I wound my way around to the hidden valley that had funneled thousands of Native Americans for thousands of years going to and from the high plains of the Montana and Wyoming buffalo grounds and the salmon fishing on the Lochsa, Clearwater, and Columbia Rivers. It was the same small valley where the Corps of Discovery had followed on the heels of the Native travelers.

I dropped off the ridge and descended into the private little valley, heading for the old Erickson cabin at the mouth of the dry creekbed.

KEEEIIAHHH! The loud screech momentarily put the fear back into me as I looked up at a large redtail hawk that suddenly took flight from its treetop perch. Unbeknownst to the dogs, I had circled back and was only a hundred yards away from them. There wasn't a yap of concern to my south as I finally relaxed and took in the scene. The historic log cabin stood at grotesque angles, rotting into the ground. An old ladder rode the cedar roof wreckage in the center of the cabin remains. Trimmed-out doors and windows were cockeyed. Square hand-hewn notches tied the remains of the structure together, keeping it afloat for now. But the wind, snow, and rain would have their way some day, the cabin slowly but surely sinking from sight into the earth. I turned around and headed up the gulch toward *Lewis and Clark Saddle*.

Hiking past another old ranch building rotting into the ground I made my way up the hidden, Eden-like ravine, with a thick forest of small-diameter Douglas fir trees erasing most of the cloud-riddled sky, and dense moss and holly-like Oregon grape plants carpeting the valley floor. Ten minutes of an easy hike along an old road turned into crashing through thick brush along an old path. It felt like I was "coming home", with ninebark and mountain maple brush whips clawing at me, my arms spreading a tunnel through the spindly branches, my feet feeling the trench of the trail that yes...*had* to be what I was looking for. "Yahoo!" I yelled into the muffling thick brush and tight canyon. I was standing on the Lewis and Clark Trail and the old Native American path that the Corps of Discovery followed! I couldn't contain my excitement. I *had* to call Judy.

"Judy, this is explorer John. Do you have a copy? Over." I listened amongst the fir trees for an answer, but only heard the wind whispering through the treetops along the ridge. To save batteries, I gave up and continued ascending the narrow ravine, spreading more brush whips as I made my way along the obvious trenched-out trail, searching for peeled trees. But I didn't spot any carved trees as the single-tread trail turned back into a double-rut road. A short distance later, the path continued straight, leaving the road that branched to the left. I stopped my advance up the ravine and contemplated which "road" to take. Without a map or Old Toby to guide me, I was on my own here. A wind wave swayed the limber fir tree tops, continuing to sing a familiar western tune as I tried to make a decision which way to go. The trench of the trail went straight up the guts of the draw. Was that the old Native trail or just a recent game and cattle trail? Figuring I was too close to the Ole Erickson cabin to go left and veer off the main fork of the drainage, I headed up the draw, following the thickly wooded path.

Soon I started picking up old gray peeled tree signs which, along with the trail trench, proved Native Americans had passed this way. Just beyond a galvanized-metal stock watering tank, I found an old trapper's cubby, made of piled-up sticks at the base of a tree. I remembered the camouflaged trap shelters on my hikes up to Lolo Peak, following Tony Zen's old trap line. He made them to protect the traps from the weather. I had used them to find my way. This trap cubby, I could tell, wasn't Tony's. It was somebody else's signature left to rot and disappear into the mountain's skin. Maybe it was one of Bud Moore's—a 1930s Woodman School alumnus and Lolo Creek valley and Lochsa River country trapper whose tracks were all over these mountains. Or possibly it was Skookum Woodman's cubby. Skookum was left at the turn of the century to fend for himself after his father and sister died of Rocky Mountain spotted fever. After the rest of the Woodman family decided to move out, Skookum stayed in the valley to trap, hunt, and fish. People would find a string of fish or a quartered deer from an unknown "stranger" left at their door, Skookum's gifts back to the people who gave him a place to stay and a meal to eat. With my find recorded by my point-and-shoot camera, I continued hiking up the depression in the tight canyon.

I figured if I was getting close to the top of the ridge at *Lewis and Clark Saddle*, the gray-blue mottled horizon would be showing more through the evergreens as I climbed higher. But strangely there wasn't any blue, or any gray. There was just the green of the trees and golden-brown of the cured hillside grasses. What was going on? Could it be that my dead reckoning was dead off? But why was I still finding carved trees if I was completely off the braids of the main Native trail?

Making my way through some more thick brush in the tightening valley floor, I finally came to a dead end at a snarled mess of tangled downfall and branches that didn't look hiker-friendly. I skirted to the right of the branch dam and scrambled up the steep ponderosa pine mountainside, discovering more Native-peeled trees as cool beads of sweat dripped down my forehead, stinging my eyes. At the top of the butt-kicking slope I rested, listening to the loud pounding of my heart. I took off my pack, wiped the sweat on my forehead, and sat down with my back against a large pine. Taking a drink from my water bottle, I gazed out from the first vista I'd had since disappearing into the woods from the valley floor, and could hardly believe what I saw. *Lewis and Clark Saddle* was perched far below me, nestled under the ridge to my south, close to a mile away! I must have taken a wrong fork in the trail. But I had followed the old carved trees. How could I have gotten lost? I looked out over the valley and of course…that was it! Clark referred to two Native American encampments, *"Some old Indian Lodges"* at the site of their *Woodman Camp* and *"an old Indian encampment"* at the mouth of Woodman Creek. The pine-studded gulches that fed into the valley were convenient peeled tree food "stores" for the Native camps, with their accompanying trails fanning out to the trees they might have cultivated like crops. I had just followed the wrong fan, which had led me too far to the north instead of due west on the main Native trail to *Lewis and Clark Saddle*.

I drank some more water, then grabbed the walkie-talkie from my pocket to let Judy know about my delay in getting to the fence finish line. "Judy…this is John. Do you have a copy?"

"John, this is Judy, go ahead!" The quick reply was weak, but readable.

"I got lost trying to find the saddle, so it will be a good two hours yet until I get down to the highway for pick up. Over."

Static… "heard you were lost, but I couldn't make out the other part."

I stood up and held the radio as high as I could, looking like a miniature Statue of Liberty. "Yeah, I got lost and it will take me at least two hours before I'll be to the highway," I practically shouted into the arm's-length-away walkie-talkie.

"I didn't copy all of that! Repeat!"

I jogged up the steep slope a hundred feet and keyed the transmitter again. "I won't be down there for a while yet!" My heart pounded like a drum.

"What? I'm not picking you up!"

"I said *baaahhh.*" The low battery sheep-in-distress signal went off. I keyed the radio again. *"Baaahhh."*

"I'm not reading you! Repeat your message!" Judy's voice blurted out of the small black box that had enough battery power to receive but not to transmit. I shoved the radio in my pocket and descended to the tree resting spot. "I'm not picking you up anymore!" Judy's coat-muffled voice sounded more frantic.

I grabbed the radio for one last try. *"Baaahhh."*

"I *still* can't hear you!"

Not wanting to ignore Judy's call, but needing to preserve what little battery power I had, I stuffed the radio back in my coat pocket. The extra batteries that I should have brought were left in my desk at *Travelers' Rest II*.

I peered down at *Lewis and Clark Saddle* again. It would have been an easy half-mile hike to the pass from the old Erickson log cabin if I had taken a left on the lower ranch road. I had already hiked well over a mile, climbed a very steep mountain, and gotten turned ninety degrees from where I wanted to go. I did have the excuse of following the peeled trees that had taken me up the wrong path. The thick tree canopy in the tight ravine on a very overcast day was another excuse. Maybe my sadness about the *Columbia* Space Shuttle tragedy was part of the cause of why my "inner compass" was off today and I had climbed at least twice as high above the valley as I intended.

"John, do you read me?" Judy's frantic voice shot out of my pocket.

I grabbed the walkie-talkie from my outside coat pocket and slipped it in my flannel shirt pocket, putting it next to my body heat to help charge it.

"John, this is Judy. I am not picking you up!"

I sat back down in the steep meadow, letting Judy's call go unanswered, patiently waiting for the batteries to recharge as I brought out Patrick Gass's journal, paging forward to the same day of the week in 1806. Sunday, February 2...

"The morning was pleasant and the weather more moderate. About the middle of the day it began to thaw and in the evening to rain."

I could feel the cold and wet of their Fort Clatsop Camp echoing through to me with the words of the past. Then I paged ahead in Patrick Gass's journal to March 18, 1806... *"making preparations to return up the river, as soon as the weather will permit."*

March 19... *"some hard showers of hail fell and it continued cloudy through the day."*

March 20... *"The whole of this day was wet and disagreeable."*

March 21... *"We had a cloudy wet morning."*

March 22... *"We had a cloudy wet morning."*

March 23... *"There was a cloudy wet morning."*

Sadly, I put away the journals and readied my pack. The trip I didn't want to end was about to come to an abrupt halt. There would be no more tomorrows of searching for Native-carved trees, cairns, historical markers, lost tread, trail braids, and flagging dancing in the wind. There would be no more sketchy stream crossings, brush shredding, or any more marathon hikes out of the Lochsa canyon to access a small amount of trail. There would be no more below-zero camping trips to discover the *Snowbank Camp,* or playing detective trying to solve the mystery of the Wendover Ridge Rest Site and Clark's desk-and-trunk wreck site. There would be no more tomorrows for using the journals to figure out where I was on the trail. Much too soon it would all be over.

Taking a mental compass bearing on *Lewis and Clark Saddle*, I started my descent. It was time to finish my trek.

Down one gully and up another, I sidehilled to reconnect with the main trail, jumping the only elk I had seen on my journey, and discovering more peeled trees. In twenty minutes I was at the saddle, standing on an old roadcut, and faced with another decision. Efficiently, I could drop into the gulch to my west and quickly get to the end-of-the-trip barbwire fence finish line. Or I could inefficiently delay the end of my trek another half hour and climb the meadow ridge to my south to check out the view and see if the walkie-talkie worked from there. It was a no-brainer. I made tracks up the hill.

"Judy! This is explorer John calling. Do you read me? Over," I spoke into the wind from the top of the ridge overlooking the valley. Delicate golden grass tassels bobbed and weaved in the late afternoon breeze.

Static. She must have heard me.

I stuck the radio back in my shirt pocket, trying to warm the batteries again as more static vibrated against my chest. The grassy hilltop stood among overlapping mountains that dove into the Lolo Creek canyon. I just stood there, mesmerized by the beauty, absorbing the special spot. The miniature white school buildings, with the school yard wrapped by the prominent white fence, looked like a scene out of *Little House on the Prairie*. The ranch houses I had passed earlier lay off to the northeast, nestled underneath me. Other isolated buildings dotted the valley floor in the distance. Although the scene had changed a little, the land remained pretty much the same since Lewis and Clark traveled through. A quick walk along the ridge showed flattened grass depressions, signs of the elk that had bedded down during the night. I felt like bedding down for the night too, and making the moment last a little longer. But I didn't have a tent or sleeping bag, or any Mountain House cuisine or pot to cook it in. Most important, I didn't have permission to camp here. The timer was almost out of sand. My trek was about to end.

After taking a self-posed timed shot, I quickly retraced my tracks to *Lewis and Clark Saddle* and reconnected with the Lewis and Clark Trail that showed as well now as at any time in my journey, leading me into a dry gulch to the west. One foot in front of another I made my way toward the fence line where I'd left off months ago. Now I was coming back to finish what I had started, connecting the thread I had woven from Travelers' Rest. The trail I was on soon faded; then after a short hunt I merged onto better-defined tread. I was on my last ascent, the final quarter mile to the fence line where my journey would be over. I slowed to a crawl, inching my way out of *No Name Gulch* to make it last, to stretch out the final distance among the darkening shadows in the last of the cloud-filtered light.

My mind started to wander as I crept like a tortoise toward the ridge. I thought back to when I was a kid dreaming about going west, and about my best next-door-neighbor childhood friend, Gary Winek, who helped nurture that dream. Gary and I were like Lewis and Clark, always looking for adventure and new country to explore. As teenagers, we hiked the Ice Age Trail near Milwaukee and biked the farm roads across Wisconsin. We traded stories around the campfire and shared dreams about doing more adventures as adults. We carried those dreams into our futures, planning treks that would continue our quest for adventure, satisfy our hunger to explore country we had never seen. Every day, in my mind, I *hiked* some new trail, *biked* some new bike path, or *sea kayaked* a lake, river or ocean. The Continental Divide Trail called, as did the Pacific Crest Trail and Appalachian Trail. Then there was the ultimate of all long-distance trails, the North Country Trail, all 7,960 miles of it from Maine to Washington. And there were more historic trails to follow: the Oregon Trail, the Sublette Cutoff, the Bridger Trail, the Bozeman Trail, and so many others. It was an obsession, in my mind and on the ground, to continue what

Lewis and Clark started when they headed west nearly two hundred years ago…exploring America.

I touched the cold steel wire, feeling the end of my reenactment journey in my fingertips. It was such a simple act with such a dramatic end. It finally was over. One of my life-long dreams was accomplished with the touch of that wire. The sign confirmed it all… *No Hunting, No Fishing, No Trespassing.*

My trek had come full circle. What I had started back in October and spent years dreaming of doing someday was finished. There was nothing more to do. The day I had lived for and the day I had dreaded *collided* into each other, making me feel so happy, but yet so sad. I took off my daypack and brought out my celebration lunch, eating my ham and cheese sandwich and drinking the Coke I had saved for the special event. I held the can of pop high in the air and toasted the Corps of Discovery. Then I reread the journals for this day in 1805 and made mental notes in mine. After a self-posed picture by the no-trespassing sign, I finished my lunch and readied my pack, the reunion with an event that happened nearly two hundred years ago finally over.

There was no sense delaying the inevitable. I had to leave now, call it a day and head back to the hilltop meadow where I would drop back down to the highway before Judy initiated a search. But I just stood there with my pack on, frozen like an ice carving at a winter carnival. I couldn't move. This spot at the barbed wire fence in a ponderosa pine park shouldn't have stalled any movement back to my other life, but it did. It was big-time stalling, procrastinating at its best. But the cold that started to freeze the sweat against my skin convinced me I had to get moving soon, before my journey once again got too much like *their* journey.

"Goodbye, Lewis! Goodbye, Clark!" I yelled into the ever-darkening tree shadows. "See you, Sacagawea!" I listened for some echoes of the past, for something that would prove they were still here. But only the wind whispered a reply.

At the Woodman Meadows overlook, I took my final break. I took off my daypack, dug into my shirt pocket for the walkie-talkie and pressed the pager button. An annoying telephone ring announced that the radio finally worked.

"Is that you, John?" Judy's relieved voice rang out over the grassy ridge.

"10-4! It's me," I spoke into the tiny black leather cased box.

"I'm waiting for you at the Elk Meadows turn-off!"

"Meet me *baaahhh!*" I lost power.

"What?" Her voice fused with the wind.

"Meet me...*baaahhh!*" Out of batteries, I was out of luck to contact Judy. Soon she would be searching up and down the valley for me. I didn't have much time left.

I peered out over the valley and gazed down on their first campsite west of Travelers' Rest. I imagined it being September 12, 1805, looking down at the Corps of Discovery, watching and waiting for them to head west from their *Woodman Camp* and travel along the toe-of-the-slope route, up the ravine and through the saddle I had named for them. Lolo Creek meandered its way through the valley floor, with cottonwoods lining its banks. I followed the winding waters to where William Clark wrote in his journal of September 11, 1805, they had *"Encamped at Some old Indian Lodges."* The words shouted through the ages to one lone person retracing their route. It was as if they were still down there, watering their horses, setting up camp, cleaning their rifles, handing out Rush's pills for the sick, portioning out some portable soup because they couldn't find any game, and discussing their next day's plans of entering the mountains. Then I replayed in my mind Clark's journal entry I had memorized so well... *"a white frost Set out at 7 oClock & proceeded on up the Creek."* After nearly two centuries I could still sense their presence—the Corps of Discovery breaking camp, moving up the wide valley against the *"hills on the right high & ruged."* I could *see* them crossing *"a Fork on the right,"* passing *"an old Indian encampment a Swet house Covered wthh earth."* Following Old Toby I could *see* the Corps *"at 2 miles assended a high hill & proceeded through a hilley and thickly timbered Countrey."* I could *hear* the sound of voices echoing across the grassy hill, erasing nearly two centuries in an instant. The clopping of the horses' hooves and the dust they caused drifted through the years as the Corps of Discovery made their way over *Lewis and Clark Saddle*.

I looked out over the valley one last time, realizing it was the journals that kept the spirit of Lewis and Clark alive. The words that were written in camp at night had spanned the ages, making me feel in a very real way that they ***were still here***, as alive today in this nation's history as ever before.

With the timer out of sand, I threw a salute to the *Woodman Camp* and stepped off the ridge, wading through the sea of golden grass, heading for home as the setting sun washed the mountains with a soft orange alpenglow.

the end

Epilogue

DECEMBER 8, 2003

The gunmetal gray sky came alive with huge pulsating waves of Canada geese migrating south, a distant loud commotion of wind-muffled honking following in their wakes. I was standing where I always felt *the west* began, on a ridge to the south of Interstate 90, overlooking the town of Chamberlain, South Dakota. Five steel bridge sections humpbacked over the Missouri River below me, leading to a rock-filled dike that connected *east* with *west*. Long snowy drapes hung in the distance, as a late-day cloud shadow lay across the grass-covered ridge I was on.

It had been nearly forty years since I had dreamed of leaving home and *going west*. Returning from another annual visit to see my parents, I was reliving the dream, following the modern-day Interstate 90 "trail" in my Nissan pickup truck, two days out of Wauwatosa and Lolo on the road that connected my two worlds.

I stared down on the wind-whipped waters of the river Thomas Jefferson had instructed Meriwether Lewis and William Clark to explore to hopefully find access to the Pacific Ocean. I sensed the Corps of Discovery's presence here as I had on my recent reenactment journey through the Bitterroots. I could *see* the keelboat, pirogues, and dugouts slowly coming into view, and *hear* the low murmur of voices echoing through the ages. If this was mid-September 1804, I would have run down and requested permission to come aboard and join them, to help pole their boats upstream, to cast off with the greatest explorers America has ever known.

My eyes were drawn skyward, distracted by the present, watching the power of nature's migrational force as the geese cut large fluctuating V's across the sky, etching dark silhouettes into the cloud-mottled gray. Maybe my "need" to go west had something to do with the natural migrating instinct of the geese that filled the sky. Maybe Americans just had *heading west* bred into them, going west from Europe and becoming pilgrims in a new land in the 1600s. It seemed to be in our national psyche to "go west", to head into the unknown to follow our spirit of adventure. I *watched* the tiny boats inching their way upstream along the blue-gray waters of the Missouri as they disappeared around a giant sweeping bend to the northwest between the folds of the low-slung dry hills in the distance.

A huge white curtain swept down across the ridge, quickly erasing the scene. I pulled my coat over my head and leaned into the wind, making my way through the blinding blizzard back along the path to continue on my journey heading west.

Bibliography

Ambrose, Stephen E. *Undaunted Courage: Meriwether Lewis, Thomas Jefferson and the Opening of the American West.* New York, Simon and Schuster, 1996.

Bergon, Frank, ed. *The Journals of Lewis and Clark.* New York, Penguin Books USA, 1989.

Crawford, John E. *The Woodman Echo.* Missoula, 1992.

Discovery Writers, The. *We Called This Creek Traveller's Rest.* Stevensville, Stoneydale Press Publishing Company, 2003.

Lolo Women's Club. *Lolo Creek Reflections.* Replication of first edition. Stevensville, Stonedale Press Publising Company, 1999.

MacGregor, Carol Lynn, ed. *The Journals of Patrick Gass, Member of the Lewis and Clark Expedition.* Missoula, Mountain Press Publishing Company, 1997.

Moore, Bud. *The Lochsa Story. Land Ethics in the Bitterroot Mountains.* Missoula, Mountain Press Publishing Company, 1996.

Moulton, Gary, E., editor. *The Definitive Journals of Lewis & Clark: Through the Rockies to the Cascades, Volume 5 of the Nebraska Edition.* Lincoln and London, University of Nebraska Press, 2002.

Salish-Pend d'Orielle Culture Committee and Elders Cultural Advisory Council Confederated Salish and Kootenai Tribes. *The Salish People and the Lewis and Clark Expedition.* Lincoln and London, University of Nebraska Press, 2005.

Space, Ralph S. *The Lolo Trail.* Second Edition. Missoula, Historic Montana Publishing, 2001.

About the author

Photo: Judy Crawford

Author John Crawford, seen here on the crest of the Bitterroot Divide near Saint Mary Peak, is an avid hiker, backpacker, mountain biker, and sea kayaker. John's spirit of adventure has led him to some of the most remote country in the continental United States, where he has followed thousands of miles of trails as a modern day explorer.

Since John's 2002 and 2003 Lewis and Clark reenactment journey, when he was forced by extreme cold and deep snows to retreat from his original goal of getting through the high country to the Weippe Prairie, he has dreamed of some day finishing his trek. Not to be denied, he picks up his Lewis and Clark quest in the fall of 2004 from the Corps of Discovery's *Snowbank Camp*, above Powell Ranger Station. He plans to write about that leg of his journey in the next book, ***Lewis & Clark and me II...The Journey West Continues***.